# Million Dollar Habits

## ALSO BY ROBERT J. RINGER

*Winning Through Intimidation*
*Looking Out For #1*
*Restoring the American Dream*

# Million Dollar Habits

## ROBERT J. RINGER

WYNWOOD™ Press
New York, New York

*T658.4*
*R58/m*
*(1)*

Library of Congress Cataloging-in-Publication Data

Ringer, Robert J.
    Million dollar habits / Robert J. Ringer.
        p.     cm.
    ISBN 0-922066-29-9 : $19.95
    1. Success in business.   2. Businessmen—Attitudes.
I. Title.
HF5386.R513       1990
658.4'09—dc20                                                    89-29399
                                                                    CIP

Copyright © 1990 by Robert J. Ringer
Published by WYNWOOD™ Press
New York, New York
Printed in the United States of America

*To my family*

*and*

*The Three Compadres,*
*Hans, Andy, and Eugenio*

# Contents

# Preface

One of the most frequent questions directed at me in seminars is, "Knowing what you know today, would you change anything in your earlier books if you had the opportunity to do so?" What a question! Of course I would. It's like asking me if I'm dead or alive. "We're all on our way to learning more," declared Don Shimoda, Richard Bach's messiah in *Illusions*. It would be difficult, if not impossible, for a person to learn and grow, yet remain static in his* thinking. While I haven't exactly become a card-carrying communist or self-immolating monk, I do strive continually to refine my basic philosophy.

An even tougher question that someone recently asked me was, "How would you define your occupation?" Interesting question, and one that, remarkably, had never before crossed my mind. After about thirty seconds, I answered, "I'm in the business of trying to make sense out of life and communicating my conclusions to others in the simplest possible manner." By at least one definition, I guess that makes me a philosopher: Someone who thinks in an effort to make sense out of life.

* Wherever the neuter is not used in this book, the masculine gender is employed for convenience purposes only. It has no other implications, implied or otherwise.

7

What a great profession! Why work for a living when you can get away with doing this? Of course, you risk going insane in the process, though I was fortunate enough to avoid such a fate until I moved to Los Angeles. It was none other than Freud himself who warned people like me, "The moment one inquires about the sense or value of life, one is sick." Even so, you know it's worth it when you check the classifieds and see what supermarkets are paying bag boys.

This book is a pretty accurate snapshot of where my thought evolution has taken me to date. To pick up my trail, just follow the path marked "Bumps, Bruises, and Scars." If you keep your eyes and brain open and move briskly, you may even avoid a number of pitfalls along the way.

Robert J. Ringer<br>
January 1, 1990

# Introduction

The first major premise of this book is that success is not dependent upon one's being blessed with superior intelligence or special skills, nor does formal education, hard work, or luck play a major role in an individual's climb toward success. The world is saturated with intelligent, highly educated, extraordinarily skilled people who experience ongoing frustration because of their lack of success. Millions of others spend their lives working hard, long hours, only to die broke.

As to breaks, they float in and out of people's lives every day without being exploited—or, in most cases, even noticed. You've undoubtedly known someone who has been the recipient of inordinately good luck, yet failed to achieve any significant degree of success. Heirs to large fortunes who are grossly unhappy, or who have lost their entire inheritances through irresponsible behavior, are classic examples of this sad phenomenon.

The second major premise of this book is that the difference between success and failure is not nearly as great as most people believe. Having personally experienced both stupendous success and colossal failure, I can state with confidence that the difference between the two is, in fact, quite slim.

The erroneous notion that there is a major difference between the actions of successful and unsuccessful people causes millions of individuals to cling to the mistaken belief that success is the result of being privy to some tenaciously guarded, mysterious secret. In the event you share this belief, I urge you to let go of it. I can absolutely assure you that there is no big secret.

This leads to the third and final major premise of this book: Success is a matter of understanding and religiously practicing specific, simple habits that *always* lead to success. Though this may not sound particularly glamorous at first blush, two realities make it quite an exciting proposition: First, it *works*. Second, habits can be learned by anyone who is willing to put forth the necessary effort.

Remember, life is nothing more than the sum total of many successful years; a successful year is nothing more than the sum total of many successful months; a successful month is nothing more than the sum total of many successful weeks; and a successful week is nothing more than the sum total of many successful days. That's why practicing simple success habits day in and day out is the most certain way to win over the long term.

Put in metaphorical terms, success is not a grand-slam home run. It's a matter of consistently hitting those dependable singles and doubles every day. The individual who makes it to the top concentrates on staying at bat and avoiding the big mistake. Then, once in a great while, the perfect pitch comes across the plate and he hits it out of the park. The important principle to grasp is that if you don't keep hitting those singles and doubles every day, you won't be at bat long enough to have the *opportunity* to hit the home run when that perfect pitch finally arrives.

In other words, you can't coast. You've got to do it *every day*.

The title *Million Dollar Habits* is a euphemism for habits that lead to positive results. Everyone gets results, regardless of the nature of his actions. A bank robber gets results. A person who refuses to work and goes on welfare gets results. An individual who is inconsiderate and rude gets results. But they aren't *pos-*

*itive* results. Keep in mind, then, that whenever I allude to *results* in this book, I'm talking about positive results—which almost without exception means results that are in your *long-term* best interest.

One final note: Though the habits I discuss in this book are relatively simple, I don't mean to suggest that it takes no effort on your part to acquire and practice them. So if all this sounds easy to you, lots of luck. I never try to sell easy. I sell what I perceive to be truth. Shall we dance?

# Chapter 1

# The Reality Habit

Reality is the foundation for every other success habit, so in order for the ideas, strategies, and information that I discuss in this book to be of maximum benefit to you, you must develop the Reality Habit. Except for an occasional accident of fate, positive results rarely find their way to people who harbor a faulty perception of reality.

Though many of the points in this chapter may seem obvious, this can create a subtle barrier, because human beings have a tendency to wave aside the obvious. Intellectually, we may agree with a point that's apparent, but when it comes time to act, we often ignore our intellect and act on emotion.

I use the word *emotion* because reality is an issue that people tend to get very emotional about. The problem is that reality is nothing more than truth, and as Baltasar Gracián, the insightful and pragmatic seventeenth-century Jesuit priest, cautioned, "Truth is abhorred by the masses." Rather than loving truth, people try to make true that which they love. Unfortunately, in the real world, this dangerous and delusive practice leads only to frustration and failure.

The fact is that most people live in a totally *unreal* world. They create a world in their own minds based on the way they would *like* the world to be rather than the way it actually *is*. All of us, to one extent or another, have adopted the philosophy of the popular humorist Ashleigh Brilliant, who once remarked, "I have abandoned the search for truth, and am now looking for a good fantasy."

People often say things like, "But this is *my* reality. Reality is different for each person." Wrong. Reality is precisely the same for everyone. There is only one reality. What differs is each person's *perception* of reality. By *perception,* I am referring to the ability to interpret correctly the events that surround you, to be able to grasp the difference between what is real and what is unreal, between fact and fiction, between what works and what doesn't work. A faulty perception of reality is almost always destructive, sometimes fatal.

It is absolutely essential that a person intellectually and emotionally understand that reality isn't the way he wishes things to be or the way they appear to be, but the way they actually *are.* The person who is not able to make this distinction finds it virtually impossible to make decisions that lead to positive results.

## Principles

As used in this chapter, a principle is synonymous with a law of Nature, as opposed to a law of man. Most man-made laws are nothing more than legalized aggression against the sovereignty of peaceful individuals, and rarely bear any relationship to natural law, reality, or moral soundness. Man-made principles, such as Parkinson's Law, are not true principles in the sense of being immutable laws. They are simply observations of human tendencies. For example, our firsthand observations lead us to conclude that expenses tend to increase as income rises.

The most significant quality of a true principle of Nature is that it can neither be created nor altered. The problem arises when people refuse to accept the reality that principles only can be discovered, and insist on believing they can create their own principles. Take the principle of gravity, for example. Isaac

Newton did not wake up one morning and decide to create a principle whereby if he dropped an apple from a tree 20 times, it would fall to the ground 19 times and go up once. Ridiculous, of course. Instead, through experimentation, he *discovered* that if you drop an apple from a tree 20 times, it will fall to the ground 20 times. What Newton did was discover the principle, or law, of gravity.

A principle, then, is the essence of reality. It is what it is, and it's up to us to discover it. To try to create our own reality is both futile and dangerous. You certainly have the right to go on believing whatever you want to believe, but reality isn't discriminatory. It will mete out negative consequences just as harshly to the well-meaning, ignorant individual as to the malevolent, stubborn person. Not once has reality excused anyone for good motives, so consistency is essential when it comes to a proper perception of reality.

## The Foundational Principle of Success

There are an infinite number of natural laws to be discovered, but fortunately you don't need a detailed understanding of every law of the universe to achieve even the most grandiose of goals. However, there is one law with which you must be totally familiar and that you must use unfailingly as a guide in all your dealings. The law I'm referring to is the ultimate, immutable law of Nature, the foundation of reality itself: Actions Have Consequences.

If I push you (an action), something must happen; i.e., there must be a consequence. You may fall down, you may stumble, or, at the very least, you will feel pressure against your body. You may also get mad at me, walk away, or push me back. The point is that I cannot escape the reality that my action, no matter how small, will have consequences. I start to invite problems into my life when I delude myself into believing that I can push you without there being any consequences at all. I am convinced that every action I have ever taken has eventually produced a predictable result.

In physics, we learn that for every action there is an equal and opposite reaction. The longer I live, however, the more convinced I am that in the daily process of living (as opposed to the science of physics), reactions tend to be *greater* than the actions that provoke them. Whenever we act improperly, the punishment seems to be way out of proportion to the "crime." My perception is that I almost always end up paying for an imprudent or unsound action over and over again, with each payment seeming to take the form of a balloon note carrying onerous, compounded interest.

The payback may take a long time, and it may be indirect or subtle in nature, but there *is* always a payback. Symbolically speaking, everything you do goes into your Book of Life. This doesn't necessarily hold a religious connotation, but I do firmly believe that universal forces are at work that pull us inexorably toward the deserving results of our actions. Kindness begets kindness; cruelty begets cruelty. Many people allow themselves to be misled because the payback for their actions often isn't immediate, which may result in their failing to make the connection when it finally arrives. Or, even when the payback is prompt, they may miss the subtlety of the connection between the results and their preceding, causal action.

Although most people probably believe the inherent truth of the principle of Actions Have Consequences, I am convinced that few people give it more than a passing thought as they go about the business of living. The question is, why? Why would we ignore such an all-powerful, immutable principle?

## A World of Delusions

To paraphrase author Robert DeRopp, man inhabits a world of delusions, which obscures reality and creates dangers for himself and others. He rarely understands what he is doing or why he is doing it. His actions and beliefs indicate that he lives in a state of waking dreams.

The most obvious motivation for one person to delude another is personal gain. In some cases, the delusion involves deceit (clandestine in nature); in others, honest overzealousness (innocent in nature). But regardless of the intent, the consequences are the same: You are deluded into believing something that isn't true. You are persuaded to ignore reality and accept an untruth in its place.

In addition to being deluded by others, there is also the problem of *self*-delusion. The results of this destructive practice can be devastating, ranging from mental illness to financial failure to war. Therefore, anyone who is serious about achieving meaningful financial results—or meaningful results of any kind—must develop the habit of carefully examining his own premises and beliefs to make certain he is not feeding himself a diet sprinkled too heavily with the spice of self-delusion.

The first step toward developing the Reality Habit, then, is to transcend our world of delusions. Delusions infest every area of life; there are no exceptions. Take the advertising business, which is the ultimate world of delusions. One might justifiably conclude that the success of most advertising is directly related to the degree to which it is able to delude the viewer, listener, or reader.

An old marketing axiom states: If you want to do well, sell people what they need; if you want to get rich, sell people what they want. How? Simple. Just invite the prospect to do something realistic like "Come to Marlboro Country." Marlboro Country, we are led to infer, is about halfway between Shangri-La and Brigadoon. Once you get there, you know you're going to be sitting atop a beautiful horse, wearing a rugged suede jacket and cowboy hat, puffing away on a lighted cigarette, looking like Robert Redford. The first step toward making all this happen, of course, is to buy a pack of Marlboros. Realistic, right?

Now, I know what you're thinking: No one possibly could be

stupid enough to be deluded by such silliness. Question: If that were true, why have cigarette companies—not to mention numerous other advertisers—been running this same type of ad for years? Certainly not because the results are so bad they're on the verge of going broke! It's because they are delightfully aware that man inhabits a world of delusions, and that it's in their financial interests to keep feeding those delusions so customers will continue to buy their products.

If you want to operate a successful advertising agency, you must remember the proven, delusionary rules of the game, such as: To sell beer, show scenes of yuppies playing touch football on the beach, jocks saying and doing illiterate things, or hard-hats engaging in stimulating activities such as welding, bulldozing, or tempering molten steel. To sell liquor, show sensual women and handsome men in tuxedos hanging around fireplaces. To sell hamburgers, show frolicking adults and children who, for no apparent reason, are giddy with laughter.

People want to smell better, look better, feel better, be more sensual, work less, make more, and play more. The fact is that people don't need beer. They don't need cigarettes. And they certainly don't need pickup trucks that go from zero to 150 miles an hour in three seconds. So what do advertisers do about this lack of need? They cleverly sell their products under the guise of what people *want*. Try to sell people what they need, and you're liable to end up in bankruptcy court.

On the other hand, *your* success is very much dependent upon *your* commitment to develop the habit of not straying too far from reality, so *you* don't become a victim of such delusions.

## Fear of Truth

In 1982, I wrote an article about the beginning of the real estate collapse which was becoming increasingly evident at the time. In that article, I said that I first began to sense the collapse was imminent when I heard a famous real estate counselor speak at a financial seminar in the summer of 1980. In response to his own rhetorical question about when the real estate bust was going to occur, he said, with a self-assured air of finality, "Ladies and gentlemen, there's no bust. There is no bust. We have a temporary lull in the market."

I didn't mention his name at the time, because I was not interested in undermining the man or debating him. I was simply astonished that a seemingly intelligent individual would make such an outrageously naïve statement, presumably knowing the facts not only about real estate bubbles, but about the history of investment bubbles in general. The simple truth is that every investment bubble bursts sooner or later. To paraphrase management guru Peter Drucker, the life span of a soap bubble averages eighteen seconds; the life span of an investment bubble averages eighteen months.

Five years later, in May 1987, the real estate wizard who made that brash statement filed for voluntary bankruptcy, listing assets of about $1 million and liabilities of nearly $3 million. I want to make it clear that I'm neither making fun of nor chastising him. My only purpose here is to warn others to be ever vigilant about the problem of self-delusion that results from a fear of truth.

What happens to most of us at one time or another is that we become so caught up in our own hype about our product or service that we simply refuse to acknowledge any facts that fly in the face of our tried-and-true sales pitch. Remember, human beings by and large don't want to hear truth. Who needs truth if it's going to put you out of business? We would much rather delude ourselves simply by ignoring the facts, even if we only succeed in prolonging the inevitable. Unfortunately, by so doing we also guarantee disastrous long-term results.

## The Something-for-Nothing Urge

The something-for-nothing urge is part of the human psyche and is based on sheer self-delusion. To one degree or another, we all possess the something-for-nothing urge. It is this urge that has made gambling a national pastime in most countries throughout history. State governments understand this all too well. They have increasingly appealed to the gambling urge to appropriate more dollars from citizens by enticing them into state-sponsored lotteries. Of course, this is in addition to the take that most states skim off the top from wagering at horse and dog tracks, jai-alai frontons, and gambling casinos. With such an explicit stamp of approval, it's little wonder that a recent survey estimated that as many as 4.2 million Americans may be addicted to gambling.

In reality, compulsive gambling is a serious mental illness that endangers both the compulsive gambler and those around him. It involves the ultimate self-delusion—the belief that something for nothing is possible, which, of course, is totally against the laws of Nature. What's so insidious about gambling is that, unlike dropping an apple from a tree, a person may actually get lucky and win now and then, which only strengthens his delusion that he can win over the long term. And it's that belief that constitutes a totally false perception of reality and brings about negative results.

## THE TURKEY MARKETS

Another prime example of delusion based on the something-for-nothing urge is to be found in the turkey markets—the Vancouver Turkey Market, the Denver Turkey Market, and the Salt Lake City Turkey Market, to name a few of the more prominent ones. The turkey markets are where "penny stocks" are traded.

If Ivan Boesky had come to Salt Lake City to ply his trade, he would have ended up parking cars for a living. Turkey-market promoters have angles that wouldn't even cross the mind of the crookedest trader on Wall Street, and gall that stretches the most larcenous of imaginations. The only reason no one's ever done a movie about the turkey markets is that moviegoers would never buy it. They would think the story was too farfetched.

The turkey markets constitute a big game of musical chairs, with the promoters of each penny stock promising to bail out their relatives and pals at a profit as soon as the next level of turkeys buy in. Of course, we all know what happens to turkeys in the end. The only question is, which ones will be left holding the fowl certificates when the music stops and there are no more buyers to be found?

A couple of years ago, when I was in New Orleans for a speaking engagement, a friend invited me to dinner with a large group of people at an elegant restaurant. I was seated next to a middle-aged attorney who not only loved to talk but also was quite inebriated. As the evening progressed, and he continued to confide in me about one sordid deal after another in which he was involved, he began talking about a penny-stock deal that he and his cronies had recently put together. As he babbled on, he kept winking and poking me with his elbow, which I misinterpreted to be uncontrollable twitches. Finally, I realized that in Cajun a wink or elbow meant, "Y'all get what ah'm sayin', ah hope."

Nervously, I began winking back and nodding my head up and down. I managed to force a smile whenever I thought my newly found confidant was expecting one, and, while focusing on his fascinating verbiage, succeeded in getting a significant portion of my meal on my suit, white shirt, and tie. Finally, the attorney simultaneously gave me a super-duper wink *and* elbowing, and, with a sinister chuckle, mumbled, "and when the stock hits the right price, the lil' old ladies end up holdin' the bag."

Ignorantly, I asked, "How do you know the price will go up? What does the company do? Is it profitable?"

The attorney looked at me with a grin that suggested I was playing games with him, and replied, "Frien', what the company does, how much it makes or loses, and what its prospects are has nuthin' whatsoever to do with the price of the stock. The price is whatever *we* say it is. All we gotta' do is open the gates when the price is right, let the lil' old ladies in, and the rest is history."

Of course, "lil' old ladies" is just a euphemism for anyone delusive enough to invest in the penny stock of a company with no track record and no perceivable future. I never cease to be amazed at the seemingly endless pool of prospective new buyers, no matter how many "60 Minutes"–type stories air on television about penny-stock scams. Only a force as mighty as self-delusion—self-delusion based on the all-powerful, something-for-nothing urge—could make it possible for such absurd scams to continue unabated.

I found out about the realities of the penny-stock game the hard way when I became involved in a "public shell." I naïvely believed I could build the company into a legitimate money-making enterprise, but the promoters of the stock had other ideas. Shortly after I jumped into the water, they began hounding me to "do something" (such as make a glitzy announcement to shareholders about the prospects of the company) to aid them in raising the price of the stock. When I steadfastly refused, they became irate and threatened to let the stock freefall. After a time, they realized my refusal was permanent, and they carried through on their threat. The result was a quick and merciful burial for the company, and, thankfully, an equally merciful end to a most distasteful and unpleasant experience for me.

You might argue that buying a penny stock isn't really the fault of the purchaser, but rather of the people who misled him with false hype about the stock in question. It's important to understand, however, that such promotions wouldn't be possible were it not for the fact that people's greed motivates them to *want* to be deluded. They practically cry out to the scammers, "Lie to me, *please* lie to me." And, rest assured, there's never a shortage of blue-suede shoers around to oblige them. If you wanted to be perverse, you might even suggest that shady penny-stock promoters provide a valuable service by telling people what they want to hear and, in the process, bursting their naïve, self-delusive bubbles. (Hmm . . . that really is perverse, isn't it?)

Regardless, the desire for something for nothing, if not kept under control, can develop into a serious case of self-delusion and completely separate an otherwise intelligent human being from the real world. It's therefore prudent to practice the habit of double-checking your premises before entering into any financial situation, making certain that you aren't being driven by a deep-seated, something-for-nothing urge.

## Delusions of Grandeur

A good example of the destructive sickness of delusions of grandeur in the business world is seen in a person who deludes himself about what he brings to the table in a negotiating situation. The person who makes this kind of mistake often ends up walking away empty-handed. If you don't have a realistic grasp of the value of your contribution to a deal, one of the most likely consequences is that serious people may refuse to deal with you. At worst, you can get yourself into a Catch-22 situation if the person you're negotiating with thinks your proposal is ludicrous. That is, in order to keep him from walking away from the deal, you might have to back down substantially, in which case the other party is likely to wonder just how much farther you might be willing to back down. And when that occurs, it puts him firmly in the driver's seat, because you've lost any semblance of posture you may have had at the outset of the negotiations.

WHATEVER HAPPENED TO . . .

We're living in an age in which professional athletes routinely demand that their contracts be renegotiated after a good year, despite being legally bound by existing contracts. (Interestingly, athletes are not willing to renegotiate their contracts *downward* after a bad year.) Sports is just another business, but because of the nature of their profession, athletes are especially prone to delusions of grandeur. They tend to overestimate their worth, so much so that it sometimes can end a career.

One of the many cases that comes to mind in this regard is that of Vince Ferragamo, a talented athlete who played in the National Football League in the late 1970s and early 1980s. After sitting on the bench for several years as a backup quarterback for the Los Angeles Rams, Ferragamo finally got his big break when the starting quarterback was injured. From the outset, Ferragamo was sensational, and the next year he led the Rams to their only Super Bowl appearance. He looked like a future Hall of Fame candidate—providing, of course, he could play at the same high level for another eight or ten years. Unfortunately, after just *one* great year, his friend, the Agent, demanded that his salary be increased to a figure many times what he was currently earning, and threatened that Ferragamo would play Canadian football in Montreal if his demands were not met.

Mistake number one was asking for more money on an already existing contract. Mistake number two was trying to get tough with Georgia Frontiere, the Rams' owner who is reputed to be worth something in the area of $1 billion. Ferragamo was guilty of failing to heed **Real-World Rule No. 187: Never push a guy who carries a big stick.** If you're nice to a gorilla, he may give you the opportunity to be clever, and you may even end up getting what you want. But if you try to play hardball with him, you're likely to get dismembered.

After Ferragamo's dismembering—he had a terrible year in Canada and came crawling back to the Rams like the proverbial puppy with his tail between his legs—he played mediocre football for the Rams for a couple of seasons, was traded to Green Bay, and soon found himself out of football. Who knows how this talented football player's career might have turned out had he simply proceeded with his career as a Ram—*as called for in his contract?*

Ferragamo's story is a great example of that ever so fine line between success and failure. Both the principle and moral are just as valid whether the business be football, real estate, or computers. Principles know no boundaries and are unable to differentiate among industries.

## THE EGOHULKSTER

The ultimate in delusions of grandeur is found in the Egohulkster, the guy who spends most of his time, energy, and money trying to convince himself and others that he's the reincarnation of Howard Hughes. A classic tip-off to the Egohulkster is lavish offices with all the trappings. Little does he know that this kind of flash serves as a red flag to experienced, successful people, particularly if the growth of his business has been unusually rapid.

A number of years ago I had dinner with an Egohulkster in his early thirties. The purpose of our get-together was to discuss a business deal we were in the process of negotiating. We never did get around to talking business, because he yapped nonstop about who he knew, how much he made, and how clever he was. At one point, apparently sensing (erroneously) that his prey's fascination had reached a fever pitch, he bellowed: "There are three things I can do around the clock—drink, gamble, and have sex." I'm telling you, I nearly yawned.

Then, with trumpets blaring inside his arthritic brain cavity, he went on to describe his awesome deal-making exploits, taking care to emphasize that he regularly flitted from coast to coast on his own Learjet. Of course, he was many years too late to impress me. About fifteen years earlier, prior to my brain transplant, I too had owned a Learjet. The truth, however, was that I had barely been able to keep up the payments on my ten-speed bicycle, let alone those on my plane. As I noted the foam dripping from the corners of the young Egohulkster's mouth, I was pretty certain that when the end arrived for him, he would lose both his Learjet *and* his bicycle. **Real-World Rule No. 52: Distrust anyone under forty with a Learjet!**

## Naïveté

Years ago my nephew, who at the time was a novice stockbroker working for a major establishment brokerage firm, said to me,

"Uncle Robert, I can't believe it. The biggest guys in the firm cheat their own clients." I smiled and assured him that he hadn't exactly discovered the Theory of Relativity. Nevertheless, self-delusion prompted by naïveté abounds among amateur stock market players. (An amateur stock market player is defined as any person who isn't involved in the stock market on a full-time basis, yet insists on "investing" in stocks.)

Understand that I'm not talking about so-called insider trading. In fact, I don't believe there is such a thing as insider trading. Insider trading is nothing more than a figment of a bunch of regulators' imaginations. In the vague sense that the term is normally used, virtually everyone who buys stocks is guilty of insider trading. That's because *all* buyers, including mythical little old ladies, buy stocks based on tips (stated or implied) that someone (usually a broker) gives them about those stocks.

So what are the Ivan Boeskys, Dennis Levines, and other heavyweight market players guilty of? The question in itself is naïve. They are, of course, guilty of ferreting out better tips! Our modern world of materialism is fueled by envy, and when you dare to play the game better than others, you run the distinct risk of going to prison.

Now, don't misunderstand me. I knew Ivan Boesky in the early 1970s when he was still just an ambitious young cobra eyeing his father-in-law's fortune. Even then he had that toothy grin that said to you from across the desk, "Trust me—just long enough for me to remove the gold inlays from your teeth," so I'm certainly not trying to paint Boesky or any other convicted market player as a saint. My only point is that, although there's nothing wrong with dabbling in the stock market, one must be careful not to delude oneself about the realities of the game— and the realities can be pretty brutal. The guys who make the serious money are smart, quick, and ruthless.

## Developing a Correct Perception of Reality

The purpose of these examples was to reinforce the point that major success comes only to those who develop the habit of avoiding the always-present, ever-tempting world of delusions. The biggest obstacle to developing this crucial, foundational success habit is that it's uncomfortable. Truth can often be harsh, and, as human beings, we quite naturally gravitate toward less pain and more pleasure. We don't like our little delusionary worlds to be upset.

However, if at times it seems inordinately difficult to refrain from embracing delusions, it's useful to remember an important principle associated with the law of Actions Have Consequences: The higher the price, the greater the benefit. The cost of a superior perception of reality is high, because the better your grasp of reality, the better the quality of your results; and the better the quality of your results, the better the quality of your life.

Thus, one of the most common reasons that so few people are consistently able to achieve meaningful results is that they are unwilling to experience the discomfort associated with relentlessly pursuing a correct perception of reality.

## Looking Inward

To acquire a correct perception of reality, you must, above all, develop the habit of being hard on yourself. You must religiously look to yourself for the cause of your problems, which means refusing to resort to transference. (In psychology, there are many definitions of *transference*. When I use the term, I'm referring to the act of looking to people other than ourselves, or circumstances perceived to be beyond our control, for the causes of our problems.)

To succeed at this task requires tremendous commitment. It also requires discipline, intellectual honesty, and a willingness to subordinate our delicate egos to the pursuit of long-term success. It means that no matter what someone else did to you, you must ask yourself what *you* could have done to avoid the problem. If you transfer responsibility for a problem to someone or something else, you are in effect telling yourself that you cannot prevent it from happening again because the problem is beyond your control. On the other hand, you can control any problem if you are willing to analyze it from the standpoint of what *you* can do to avoid its recurrence.

## A LITTLE FIST FOR THE CAMERA, PLEASE

A prime example of what I'm referring to happened to me shortly after my first book hit the best-seller lists. When I changed the original title of my book, *A Brutal Experiment in Business Reality*, to *Winning Through Intimidation*, I hadn't given the slightest thought to the long-term consequences of my actions. I changed the title for one reason and one reason only: to gain the public's attention in the hope of increasing sales. To that end, it certainly was a success, but there's one little problem I forgot about: *Actions have consequences.*

*Winning Through Intimidation*, which is a book about how to *defend* yourself against intimidating people, is precisely the kind of brash fuel for which mass-circulation publications scour the countryside. Since the editorial morticians who work for these publications have neither the time nor the desire to read the books they write about (or, for that matter, to investigate responsibly *most* of the things they write about), once *you* make your bed, they obligingly put you to sleep in it. Viewing the matter in this light, and considering all the juicy material I furnished them, you'd think that the least the media would do is send me a card on Machiavelli's birthday each year.

Early on, I had an inkling of what was to come for the remainder of at least one lifetime. *Time* magazine wanted to do a feature story about Robert Ringer and "the *Winning Through Intimidation* phenomenon," and the reporter writing the article said she needed a new photograph of me to go with the story. I agreed to allow her to send a photographer to my office, which resulted in about two hundred pictures of me in a variety of poses. With that many shots to choose from, I fully expected *Time* to select one that made me resemble Tom Selleck.

No such luck. The dice had been loaded from the start. When the shooting session began, the photographer said to me, "Why don't we try to loosen you up a bit first. Just let it all hang out and make some funny faces. Here, let's see you make a fist—like this [demonstrating what he had in mind]. Yeah, that's good—a fist. Great! Now, just for the fun of it, how about a few menacing facial expressions [again demonstrating what he had in mind]. I've found this kind of kidding around helps to reduce tension and makes for a better shooting session."

Without giving it much thought, I tried to relax and go along with the "loosening up" portion of the picture-taking session, joking with the photographer and making a fist and some contorted faces for him. Little did I know that the rest of the shooting would be purely cosmetic, because he had already gotten the pictures he was after.

Within a couple of weeks, there I was in *Time,* sporting a menacing sneer and clenching my left fist. I just happened to be looking to my left in the center of a two-page spread, and abutting my picture on the adjacent page was a picture of Michael Korda, the author of *Power! How To Get It, How To Use It,* looking to his *right.* He, of course, was clenching his *right* fist and staring ominously "at me."

I'm sure there wasn't a *Time* reader in the country who didn't assume that Korda's and my pictures had been taken together and that we willingly—even eagerly—had posed that way for the article. The truth? Korda and I never even met each other until we appeared together on the Donahue show about six months after those pictures appeared in *Time.* Nevertheless, there we were, two obvious bad guys making fists at each other and flaunting our evil ways. A nice little piece of photo editing, to say the least. Fraudulent, yes, but clever . . . very clever. The content of the story, needless to say, was even more misleading.

Now, I sometimes tend to display a soft-alloy brain—very malleable—so instead of regrouping and rationally assessing the long-term consequences of my actions, I ignorantly stumbled from one situation to another as the Ringer-the-Intimidator image caught on. *People, Us, The New York Times,* and local newspapers coast to coast seemed to relish every opportunity to embellish this image. Though the false hype irritated me, the resulting sales of the book were gratifying, so I continued to conform to the bad-guy role the media had assigned to me.

It would have been easy for me to spend the rest of my life complaining that the media had treated me unfairly. However, after the initial shock wore off and I was able to take the time to analyze the situation objectively, honesty compelled me to admit that the media wasn't the culprit. It wasn't the media who had renamed my book *Winning Through Intimidation*, nor had the media put a gun to my head and forced me to do interviews under their conditions. The power of choice always had been mine, and I had chosen not to assess rationally the long-term consequences of my actions. The resulting balloon note was a kind of permanent open season on "Ringer the Intimidator," not only by the media but also by a number of self-righteous writers and speakers who jumped at the opportunity to take potshots at me in a shameless effort to puff up their own phony images.

## Big Picture/Little Picture

The most common example of transference that I see in the business world is in people who spend years believing that if only so-and-so hadn't deceived or defrauded them, they wouldn't be broke today. This kind of faulty perception of reality can spread like a cancer and result in a lifetime of failure if allowed to go unchecked. On the other hand, an inward-looking response can pave the way for a lifetime of positive results. A healthy, nondelusive reaction to someone's cheating you would be to immediately ask yourself what *you* could do to avoid dealing with this type of individual in the future. The solution to a great many of your problems may be simply to improve your reading of people. And guess what? That's something *you* can control. Such a solution isn't dependent upon others changing—which is no small point, because they almost never will.

You might say that the Little Picture is that someone cheated you, but the Big Picture is to learn how to spot and avoid such a person in the future. To the extent an individual becomes adept at the latter, he escapes his waking-dream state and begins making strides toward entering the real world. As one continues to study the Big Picture, he becomes increasingly adept at being able to observe trends in human behavior, trends that will tell him what he needs to know to avoid or successfully resolve an infinite array of problems that stalk every person throughout life.

## The Search for Truth

It can't be repeated too often: Reality is nothing more than truth. Therefore, the search for an accurate perception of reality is nothing less than a search for truth. One reason that people have differing perceptions of truth is that we all start from our own set of assumptions. Thus, the serious seeker of truth must learn to question everything and be willing to give up cherished notions, even if it means suffering discomfort.

Where does the search for truth begin? Truth is to be found in knowledge and wisdom, the keys to understanding how the world works. Knowledge and wisdom are the building blocks of an accurate perception of reality, and the nice thing about these building blocks is that they can never be taken from you.

Knowledge can be gained through reading, the verbal teachings of others, and even (believe it or not) substantive television programs. The more facts you know about the world, the better are your chances of understanding how it works. Unfortunately, very few people are willing to commit the necessary time and effort to acquire any significant amount of knowledge, as evidenced by the fact that only about 3 percent of the population own library cards.

Wisdom, however, is even more important than knowledge when it comes to understanding how the world works. Wisdom might properly be defined as common sense, or good judgment.

It's easy to observe the truth in the maxim "Knowledge without wisdom is useless," because, as alluded to in the Introduction, the world is saturated with highly educated derelicts who are neither happy nor financially successful.

## LEARNING THROUGH THE EXPERIENCE OF OTHERS

Another maxim with which you are undoubtedly familiar is "Only a fool learns through his own experience, but the wise person learns through the experience of others." Obviously, learning through the experience of others is a far more efficient way of gaining wisdom, because you avoid wasting all the time, energy, and expense normally associated with learning from your own experience.

The shortest route to success in any field of endeavor, and life in general, is to seek the company of those who have a great deal of wisdom. It simply makes good sense to get in the habit of surrounding yourself with wise people. One very effective way to do this is to read the works of the great philosophers. This allows you to tap into a huge reservoir of wisdom that no single individual can offer. Alfred Korzybski, the renowned semanticist, described this phenomenon as "time binding," the recording of an experience and passing it on to others.

Unfortunately, no person on earth takes full advantage of the opportunity to learn through the experience of others. In fact, the actions of some people have prompted me to pen the **Contrarian Common-Sense Syndrome: Some people consistently do the exact *opposite* of whatever the empirical evidence suggests would be the wisest course of action.** Perhaps you're acquainted with someone who's a victim of this syndrome, and have wondered why anyone would take such a self-destructive approach to life. It's an interesting question to ponder. It could be that the person wants to prove that he's smarter than those who have already experienced a similar situation; or that he doesn't really believe that he deserves success; or it may just be a case of his being belligerent. It's simply one of those great mysteries of life that defies explanation.

Children have an especially acute problem of refusing to learn through the experience of others. Because of their inexperience, children don't have enough wisdom to understand that the easiest way to *obtain* wisdom is to learn through the experience of others. As a result, the Contrarian Common-Sense Syndrome can be seen in a disproportionate percentage of those passing through the Age of Infinite Wisdom. The Age of Infinite Wisdom is that blissful period of life during which a person knows *everything,* the unfortunate result being that his mind is pretty much closed to advice. Since he already possesses infinite wisdom, no one— whether he be Socrates or your average parent—can contribute much to his seemingly saturated mental bank.

Passing through the Age of Infinite Wisdom is a perfectly normal part of the maturation process, providing it doesn't drag on for an inordinate number of years. In many cases, however, a person may remain stalled in the Age of Infinite Wisdom well into his thirties, forties, or even beyond, which usually results in his continuing to act like a child long after he has become a chronological adult. Such an adult refuses to take advice from people wiser than he, and can never seem to figure out why he continually self-destructs.

The wise person works hard at learning through the experience of others, because he has a sincere appreciation for the efficiency of such a sound habit.

## Learning Through Your Own Experience

Even if an individual wants to, it's impossible to learn all he needs to know through the experience of others. Like it or not, each of us must gain most of our wisdom through our own experience. There's nothing wrong with this, provided a person doesn't repeatedly make the same mistakes. The longer it takes someone to learn through his mistakes, the more he runs the risk of making the Big Mistake—the mistake that can cause irreversible damage, or damage serious enough to have a major, negative impact on his life over a long period of time.

A person must acquire the habit of extracting the lesson learned from each negative experience, then applying his new-found wisdom to future experiences. Ideally, your habit in this area should become so strong that when you make a mistake you instinctively and immediately think of totally unrelated situations in which correction of the underlying cause of the mistake you've just made could be applied to your benefit.

## Dreams Versus Reality

Though the development of a correct perception of reality is not an easy task, due in no small part to our being surrounded by a world of delusions, the nice thing about it is that you get better with practice, provided you are committed to truth. This means being willing to subordinate your desires and wishes—your dreams, as it were—to reality. That is not to say that you should not have dreams. On the contrary, dreams are important. What it does mean, however, is that you should not allow your dreams or desires to override reality. In other words, your love of truth must be greater than your desire to make your dreams come true.

The more often, and more quickly, you are able to recognize truth in your day-to-day encounters in the Businessworld Arena—and in life in general—the more likely you will be to escape the customary human state of waking dreams. When you correctly perceive reality, delusions begin to disappear. And as delusions vanish from your life, you are able to deal effectively with problems on a more rational basis, which in turn leads to high-level success.

As you continue to read, keep in mind that the Reality Habit is the foundation for every other Million Dollar Habit discussed in this book. Therefore, in order for the ideas, strategies, and information presented in the following pages to be of maximum benefit to you, it is vitally important that you master this foundational habit.

# Chapter 2

# The Attitude Habit

SALT LAKE CITY, DECEMBER 3, 1969 . . .

As we began our final descent, the control tower operator—who later testified that he had been on duty for sixteen hours without a break and, in addition, was nursing a bad case of the flu—told us that we were two miles behind a Frontier Airlines 737 jet. Unfortunately, the truth was closer to two thousand feet—practically on top of it! Suddenly, our Learjet was caught in the backwash of the Frontier jetliner in front of us. It was like being hit by a tornado, and it nearly turned our small aircraft upside down.

Frantically, my chief pilot, Walt, shouted to the tower, "Negative on the go-round," in response to instructions for Learjet 714-XJ to lift its nose and circle again before attempting to land. I looked up and saw the earth rushing toward us through the cockpit window. Too late to pull the nose up. The plane was almost upside down, and my five companions and I were about to crash!

The thought flashed through my mind that I had always wondered what it would feel like just before the final moment arrived. "Would I be conscious of suffering, or would it be so quick and complete that I wouldn't even know what had happened?" I wondered. In an instant, I was about to find out.

Miraculously, Walt managed to keep the aircraft from landing upside down, but we hit at a right angle to the ground. It seemed as though we remained balanced on the tip tank of our right wing for an eternity, screeching along at 100-plus miles an hour with Walt struggling to keep the plane from flipping over on its back. Finally, the plane fell toward its underbelly and began spinning wildly in circles off to the side of the runway.

I looked down and saw gravel and dirt through gaping holes in the floor of the aircraft. Flames were shooting into the cabin as we continued to rotate like a runaway top. It's amazing how many clear thoughts can be crammed into a thimble of time when you're in a life-and-death situation. Only someone who has experienced a similar kind of disaster can fully appreciate what I mean. It's as if you instantly shift into a superconsciousness that many have described as seeing their whole life flash in front of them.

I'll never know for sure how many times the Learjet spun around before it came to a halt in the muck adjacent to the runway, but it seemed like at least ten or fifteen. What I do remember is that the wheels had been torn off and the floor was almost completely gone. A single thought dominated my mind as the cabin quickly filled with fire and smoke: Explosion! And instant extinction for me and the others trapped inside.

Then came those exhilarating, lifesaving words from the co-pilot, Ron: "Emergency door!" Richard, one of my assistants who happened to be sitting in the rear seat adjacent to the emergency exit on the right side of the plane, grabbed the emergency handle and ripped the door out. All I remember thinking was that if I hurled my body through the opening quickly enough, I might have a chance to live, while a slower exit might mean death.

Without giving it a second thought, I dove out of the plane headfirst, landing like a sack of potatoes on the mixture of gravel, dirt, snow, and sleet outside. I was in my stocking feet, but who cared? Instinctively, I jumped up and began mimicking a world-class sprinter. "Got to get as far away from the explosion as possible" was my only thought as I huffed and puffed like the out-of-shape porker I really was.

After running about seventy-five yards, I dropped to the ground in exhaustion. I was cold and wet, but never mind that. I was alive and breathing, torn clothes and all, sitting on the frozen ground and witnessing my toy turn into an $800,000 bonfire.

I watched my copilot crawl through the emergency exit, then held my breath waiting for Walt to follow. Two seconds, five, ten . . .

Again an eternity, but no Walt. My gosh, Walt was going to get blown to pieces in front of my eyes! There's no way I can describe the feeling of helplessness I experienced during those tense seconds. Should I run back and try to save him, John Wayne style? I pictured the next day's headlines blaring: **Jerk Entrepreneur Blown to Bits in Clumsy Effort to Save Pilot.**

Fortunately, before having to make such a life-and-death decision, Walt appeared in the emergency exit, climbed out, and ran over to me. I was still sitting on the ground, arms on knees, when he stopped in front of me. The first words out of his mouth were, "You probably don't realize it, but I just saved your life." (Ron later told me how the plane had come within a hair of flipping on its back when we were skidding along on our right wing tip, and how Walt had had the presence of mind to fight the steering wheel like a rodeo cowboy atop a bull, refusing to let up until he had persuaded the out-of-control plane to come to a halt right side up. Ron told me that had we flipped over, it would have meant certain doom for us.)

It was nothing short of miraculous. The plane had been totaled, but, save for a few scratched knees, all six people aboard were uninjured. It seems strange now, but as I sat and watched the emergency fire crews battling the blaze, I didn't give much conscious thought to the fact that I had just survived a plane crash. It's wonderful being young and stupid. Life's eternal. Why *shouldn't* I survive a plane crash?

## LOS ANGELES, DECEMBER 1, 1982 . . .

A twenty-nine-year-old entrepreneur awakens before dawn to meet the challenge of a new day. Across town, a house painter goes through much the same ritual. The two men do not know each other, but, without realizing it, they will soon meet.

The young man heading east in a late-model Datsun and the painter traveling south in a Toyota pickup truck are destined to become participants in a million-to-one shot. At approximately 6:30 A.M., just as the early morning sky is beginning to reveal a hint of color on the horizon, they arrive at a major Los Angeles intersection at precisely the same instant. Had either of them taken just one second longer to brush his teeth, put on his shoes, or start his car, he would have missed his catastrophic appointment with destiny. Unfortunately, the timing is perfect and the two men end up on the wrong side of the law of averages.

According to later accounts, both parties were traveling at speeds of at least 35 miles an hour, and because it was so early in the morning there were no other cars to impede their progress. Also, the traffic light at the intersection was inoperative as a result of a severe windstorm the previous night.

One of the paramedics who arrived shortly after the accident told me he was certain the young man never knew what happened, because the Datsun left no skid marks. The pickup truck had slammed into it broadside without braking. The investigating officer told me it was one of the worst city-street collisions he had ever investigated.

The young man whose life had ended so abruptly had been intelligent, hard-working, and ambitious, with a great future ahead of him. Then, without warning, it was all over. On December 3, 1982, thirteen years to the day after I had survived a Learjet crash, we buried my nephew, Michael Press.

# Randomness?

The question is, why do some people, against seemingly impossible odds, escape death, while others, with the odds heavily weighted in their favor, become victims? It's a difficult puzzle for mere mortals to understand. Are cynics right in their contention that life is random? The question of whether or not man possesses the power to control his destiny—and, if so, to what extent—has been debated throughout history.

Many people are absolutely convinced that life is random. One of their most common "proofs" is to point to the fact that so many seemingly undeserving and/or incompetent people stumble into positions of great wealth and power. Why is one man born Prince Charles and another an Ethiopian peasant?

Consciously or unconsciously, people who see life as random believe in one of two theories. The first is "quietism," which is the belief that the past, present, and future are illusions of our consciousness, but that in reality they are one and the same. In this view of the universe, nothing can be changed; everything is permanent. In other words, there's no sense trying to better one's existence, because our future existence is already history.

I refer to the second theory as the Big Bang Predestination Theory. This view of the universe holds that everything that has been, is, or will be said and done throughout history was precisely determined 14 billion years ago by the nature of the Big Bang, the initial explosion that scientists generally agree was the beginning of today's known universe. At the first instant of that spectacular eruption, every atom was sent flying on an eternal voyage that was predetermined by the intricacies of the explosion's impact. Again, this is a theory that reflects the belief that nothing can be changed by anybody or anything. Every detail of every event has already been set on an unalterable course.

Predestination advocates believe that if you say, "But I can *decide* to pick up this saltshaker right now if I want to," not only is your free will to make such a decision an illusion, but so, too, is your belief that you are acting out of free will; i.e., even your perception that you made a decision was predetermined 14 billion years ago. They believe that the Big Bang propelled into the universe the atoms that formed your brain in such a way that it would think it was making that decision today. Likewise, this one-time megablast spewed out the atoms that formed your vocal cords in such a way as to express those words today, as well as the atoms that formed your hand in such a way as to pick up the saltshaker today.

## Human Intervention

Billionaire J. Paul Getty was once asked to write a magazine article on how he became so rich, to which he responded, "Some people find oil. Others don't." Talk about playing into the hands of randomness advocates. Okay, I acknowledge that luck plays at least some part in the way events turn out. In fact, I admit there's a *lot* of luck involved. However, I'm just as convinced that luck isn't the only factor in the life equation, and that it would be extremely unwise to leave your destiny in the fickle hands of luck.

The law of averages determines the long-term inevitability of things; i.e., it establishes odds. But here's a fascinating thing about odds: If you flip a coin one time, the odds are 50–50 that it will come up heads. So if you flip a coin 20 times and it comes up tails 20 times in a row, what do you think the odds are that it will come up heads the twenty-first time? Would you believe the odds are still only 50–50? It's true. Ask any mathematical probabilities expert. The odds that heads *ultimately* will come up 20 more times than tails, and thus eventually catch up and come in line with the 50–50 ratio, are 100 percent. But the odds on *any one flip of the coin* are still only 50–50.

However, when it comes to the human experience, there's an important additional factor to consider. Human beings, unlike any other species, are much more than just conscious creatures. Human beings can plot, plan, conceptualize, and even will things to happen. Unlike the flipping of a coin, human beings have the capacity to alter events. For example, a human being can decide *not* to flip the very coin in question. He has the power of choice. He can decide to drive slower, and thus lessen his chances of being on the wrong side of the law of averages. He can decide not to smoke, and thereby decrease his chances of dying of lung cancer. He can decide which business deals to work on in an effort to improve his odds of success. He can decide to stay single, or get married, or go skiing, or just hide under his bed. And whatever decisions he makes, whatever his choices, will have a great deal to do with *his* odds versus the inevitable, overall odds dictated by the law of averages.

To be sure, randomness and inevitability will always take their toll. But you have been given the power to intervene, to affect the odds in *your* specific case. William James was unequivocal on this point when he stated, "The greatest revolution of our generation is the discovery that human beings, by changing the inner attitudes of their minds, can change the outer aspects of their lives."

I thought about James's quote when I read Viktor Frankl's remarkable book *Man's Search for Meaning*. Frankl is a world-renowned Austrian psychiatrist who has followed in the bigger-than-life footsteps of fellow Austrians Freud and Adler. All told, he has written some twenty-eight books, lectured on almost every continent, been a guest faculty member at prestigious universities throughout the world, and has received numerous honorary degrees.

An impressive vitae, to be sure. Yet the most remarkable thing about Viktor Frankl is that the majority of his accomplishments came after he had spent three horrifying years in the Nazi concentration camps of Auschwitz and Dachau. In *Man's Search for Meaning*, Frankl describes, in vivid detail, the trauma, degradation, and suffering he endured during his incarceration by the Nazis. He describes trudging through snow, ice, and mud, with no socks on his feet and frostbitten toes sticking through holes in his shoes. He recounts how the Nazis tormented him, beating him and hitting him on the back of the head with their rifle butts, and what it was like to witness friends and relatives stuffed into gas chambers or buried alive. Then, at the end of each brutal, agonizing day, sick from the pangs of starvation, he and his fellow prisoners would be given a cup of watered-down soup—with a single pea at the bottom of the cup—as their daily ration. He tells of even having to sleep in his own excrement.

To be sure, this kind of suffering is beyond the comprehension of most of us. So when someone who has endured such a living nightmare—particularly an individual of Frankl's stature—reflects on his experiences, his words carry a great deal of credibility. And perhaps the most fascinating reflection of all by this remarkable man who managed to survive such indescribable torture is his statement, in *Man's Search for Meaning*, that "everything can be taken from a man but one thing: the last of the human freedoms—to choose one's attitude in any given set of circumstances, to choose one's own way."

Throughout *Man's Search for Meaning*, Frankl makes it clear that attitude was an essential, shared element among those who survived Auschwitz and Dachau. I was so impressed with Frankl's emphasis on attitude as the key to his survival that it prompted me to take a closer look at the phenomenon commonly referred to as "positive mental attitude." (When Frankl speaks of attitude, the word *positive* obviously is implied; e.g., "positive attitude," or the more commonly used phrase, "positive mental attitude," also known as "PMA.")

I am still of the opinion that most people who expound the virtues of maintaining a positive mental attitude do not themselves really understand its nature. When I was much younger, I was very cynical about people who advocated PMA, because those who most vociferously promoted its powers often seemed to be advocating a superficial, plastic approach. I could never buy the idea that a person could achieve positive results simply by grinning from ear to ear and telling himself, "I'm great! I'm great! I can do it! I can do it!"

Worse, I noted that this approach often backfired over the long term. The problem is that if a person merely smiles and makes superficial proclamations about his attitude, or paints on a happy face and inundates associates with positive statements, a failure likely will cause him to become skeptical about the value of PMA.

There are only five human wills: the will to power, the will to pleasure, the will to meaning, the will to self-transcendence, and the will to death. You cannot will such feelings as hope, love, or belief. In other words, those who advocate motivational chants—"Just fake it till you make it" is a common one that comes to mind—succeed only in leading a lot of uninformed, naïve people down a path to inevitable failure and frustration. To sustain a *true* positive mental attitude—to embrace permanently what I call the Attitude Habit—you must do more than emotionalize; you must *intellectualize*. By *intellectualize*, I mean you have to analyze and understand exactly what PMA is, and how and why it works.

First, let's dispel the notion that there's anything magical about the term *positive mental attitude*. It's neither esoteric nor mystical. You could just as well call it a "good attitude," a "positive outlook," or a "healthy view." But regardless of the name you give it, the foundation for achieving and maintaining a positive mental attitude is belief. When you say of someone, "Boy, does that guy ever have a positive mental attitude," you're really saying, "Boy, does that guy ever have strong belief."

Plain and simple, PMA without belief is nothing more than playacting, and at the first sign of trouble you can be sure it will desert the actor. No matter how much you insist that you can accomplish something, your insistence doesn't make it happen. What counts is action, and only a person with strong belief is likely to take action. An individual may claim to believe he can succeed in another field of endeavor, yet at the same time complain that he can't quit his present job because of financial obligations. The fact that he is not willing to risk the loss of current income demonstrates a *lack* of belief, and his so-called PMA turns out to be nothing more than empty words. What he's really saying through his inaction is, "Golly, I might fail, and then what would I do?" Belief, then, is an essential component of the Attitude Habit.

## Acquiring the Real Thing

If belief cannot be willed, how does one acquire it? The same way one achieves an understanding of the way the world works: through the attainment of knowledge and wisdom. The greater your knowledge and wisdom, the stronger your belief.

Again, by *knowledge* I am referring to the accumulation of specific information; by *wisdom*, I'm simply talking about insight, or common sense. If you think in terms of a specific project or line of work, it's obvious why knowledge and wisdom lead to belief. After all, the more you know about an undertaking or profession, the more confident you tend to be. But to achieve and maintain an overall positive mental attitude requires a much broader base of knowledge and wisdom. Specifically, it requires a solid understanding of the way the world works, as discussed in Chapter 1.

This is a vast subject, because there are an infinite number of basic principles and universal laws. However, I don't think it's necessary to be all-knowing in order to achieve and maintain a strong PMA. In fact, I've come to the conclusion that if you have a clear understanding of just four basic realities, you should be able to sustain the Attitude Habit throughout life.

**Reality Number One: Problems are an integral, ongoing part of the living experience.** I don't like this any better than you do, but I'm convinced that a Pollyanna-like outlook on life is an invitation to disaster. If you see every obstacle as a totally unexpected occurrence, it's easy to delude yourself into believing that you are simply the victim of bad breaks. Then you don't have to do anything about it, because victims don't act; their main focus is on being bitter and complaining. Better to accept the reality that life is full of difficulties and dilemmas so you can focus your time and energy on becoming adept at resolving those difficulties and dilemmas as quickly and easily as possible.

In other words, when you intellectually and emotionally grasp the reality that problems are a way of life, you put yourself in the proper frame of mind to adapt to negative situations and maximize them to your benefit. To do this takes *genuine* PMA, and realizing that life is fraught with problems actually strengthens, not weakens, your belief.

**Reality Number Two: The Natural Law of Balance.** The Natural Law of Balance is pretty much synonymous with Emerson's Law of Compensation. Simply put, the universe is in balance. We see it at work all around us: electrons and protons; night and day; male and female; hot and cold; life and death; two sides to a coin. Where this law comes into play in daily life is in our having to come to grips, sooner or later, with the reality that we can't have our cake and eat it, too. Nothing is one way: for every positive, there's an offsetting negative; for every negative, there's an offsetting positive.

You should never delude yourself about the reality that you must always give up something in order to gain something. If you can't see one or more offsets when making a decision, you'd best call time out and study the situation more carefully, because it probably means that you're overlooking one or more important facts. To ignore offsetting balances is to ignore reality, which always leads to bad long-term results.

Why is an understanding of the Natural Law of Balance so critical to the foundation of a strong belief? Because it gives you the mind-set needed to look quickly and automatically for the offsetting positive in every negative situation, which is what PMA is all about. You could make an excellent case for every negative occurrence being nothing more than an illusion hiding something of value to you. Speaking of illusions, Richard Bach put it eloquently in his book of that title when he said, "What the caterpillar calls the end of the world, the Master calls a butterfly."

You've heard this theme many times before in such expressions as "Every failure plants the seed of an equivalent success" and "Always look for the half-full glass rather than the half-empty glass." People who think this way are not blind optimists. Rather, they simply understand that there's an equal and offsetting positive to every negative situation, so they immediately look for positives as soon as something goes wrong. I like to refer to this habit as "maximizing the positives in negative situations."

One outstanding example involved a wheeler-dealer attorney friend of mine who had for years straddled the fence between practicing law and being an entrepreneur. He was forever lamenting about the degradation of having to practice law (you've got to love an attorney who's that candid), and was frustrated because his law practice bogged him down in time-wasting detail. He was the sole proprietor of his firm, which included about thirty attorneys and staff members. It was an energy-draining, high-overhead situation that continually stifled his beloved entrepreneurial pursuits.

Suddenly, his whole life seemingly fell apart. He was indicted on a bribery charge relating to a cable television franchise he had worked on for one of his clients. Though he adamantly proclaimed his innocence throughout the trial, to his disbelief he was convicted and sentenced to serve about three months in a minimum-security federal prison. As a result, he was disbarred, lost about half his net worth fighting legal battles, and saw his previously pristine reputation and most of his friends disappear. His law firm, for all practical purposes, was forced to shut down because of the black cloud hanging over his head, and on the surface his future looked hopeless. His life was in shambles, but he fiercely believed in his innocence. Ultimately, his belief paid off and his conviction was overturned on appeal.

The offsetting positive? Ironically, the result of all this devastation was that he was finally able to devote full time to the entrepreneurial side of his life, something he had wanted to do for years. The cataclysm that had befallen him quickly accomplished what he himself had not been able to do: close down his law practice and escape the high-overhead, high-energy drain that went along with it.

By being relieved of his law-office millstone, he was able to double his already substantial net worth within a relatively short period of time. And, best of all, he was able to escape the humiliation of having to practice law! Incredible, isn't it? What could be worse than having twenty-five years of hard work, of building an impeccable civic reputation, go down the drain because of an accusation that the courts ultimately ruled to be untrue? Yet, by ferreting out the seed of an equivalent success in the misfortune that had befallen him, he actually succeeded in dramatically improving the career and financial aspects of his life. It was a classic example of practicing the habit of maximizing the positives in a very negative situation.

**Reality Number Three: The law of averages.** The law of averages, which I briefly touched on earlier in this chapter, can be applied to just about every facet of life. Insurance companies use it to compile actuary tables, sports teams keep statistics on all phases of their games, and gambling casinos put the fate of their enterprises totally in the hands of the law of averages, which never fails them over the long term.

An understanding of the law of averages is essential to the maintenance of the Attitude Habit, and thus to financial success. If you try to put a deal together 20 times, your chances of succeeding, all other things being equal, are twice as good as if you tried only 10 times. And if you try 40 times, your chances of succeeding are 4 times as great as if you tried only 10 times. Now if that sounds simplistic, the question is, why doesn't everybody apply this universal law by making it a regular practice to keep on trying until he succeeds? Answer: Most people don't really understand and/or believe that the law of averages will work for them over the long term.

That's pretty amazing when you consider that just about everybody has read or heard about numerous success stories in which it's clear that the law of averages played an integral part in the individuals' ultimate triumphs. Colonel Sanders supposedly approached over one thousand restaurants before he finally succeeded in getting one to carry his chicken recipe on its menu. It's been said that Thomas Edison tried more than ten thousand different light bulbs before he made one that worked. And Abraham Lincoln's story is legend: Over a period of twenty-eight years, Lincoln lost his job, failed in business, suffered a nervous breakdown, and was defeated numerous times for public office—until he finally won the election that made him president of the United States!

The law of averages works in conjunction with the Natural Law of Balance, assuring that it's just a matter of time until the offsetting positive to any negative occurrence makes its appearance.

**Reality Number Four: Through the power of the mind, it's possible to exert a great deal of control over your destiny.** Interesting, isn't it? Problems are inevitable, yet through the power of your mind you have the capacity to help determine your destiny.

When Napoleon Hill, in *Think and Grow Rich*, first penned such statements as "Anything the mind can conceive and believe, it can achieve" and "When you're ready for a thing, it will make its appearance," he based his beliefs on centuries of empirical evidence drawn from human experience. But as modern scientific research has rapidly accelerated its pace, creditable cases, such as Norman Cousins's well-publicized recovery from a diagnosed terminal illness, gained more and more attention. Cousins, as you probably are aware, describes his amazing mind-power cure in his best-selling book, *Anatomy of an Illness*. Cousins had a friend bring a movie projector to his hospital room, and spent months watching hilarious movies like those of the Marx

Brothers, literally laughing himself out of his disease. What's particularly impressive about his case is that the medical profession is pretty much in agreement that Cousins's mental state was the crucial determinant in his overcoming his "incurable" illness.

In recent years, scientific researchers have made even more dramatic strides in discovering the major role that the mind plays in producing results. Of particular interest is the work done by Dr. Karl Pribram, a Stanford University neurosurgeon who has convincingly demonstrated that there is a direct correlation between what the mind visualizes and the results a person achieves. Dr. Pribram's Theory of Holographic Memory contends that the mind houses three-dimensional holographic images of what it envisions, which in turn stimulates the senses to translate those images into their physical, real-life equivalents. More precisely, when your mind believes something to be true, it stimulates your senses to draw to you the things, people, and circumstances necessary to convert the mental image it houses into its physical reality.

Thus, there is nothing at all mystical about the power of the mind and its ability to control its owner's destiny. On the contrary, it's a phenomenon that is scientific in nature. Therefore, the individual who aspires to a permanent positive mental attitude would be wise to do sufficient studying to convince himself of the reality that the powers of the mind can, in fact, draw to him the things, people, and circumstances necessary to convert his desires into results.

Based on the evidence, you might say that a good way to start getting what you want is to develop the habit of imagining that you already have it. For example, let's go back to Napoleon Hill's statement, "When you're ready for a thing, it will make its appearance." Have you ever heard something for years, then suddenly the right person, in the right place, at the right time says it in just the right way, and you say, "Wow, that's great—what a terrific thought!" Then a friend or spouse says, "But I've been telling you that for years, and you've never gotten excited about it before. What's the big deal?"

The big deal is that prior to that time you had not been ready for it. You never before had really believed it and clearly pictured it. When it finally hit you like a sledgehammer, it was because you were ready to hear it, ready to absorb it, ready to act on it, so it created the illusion that it magically made its appearance at that particular moment.

## Expansive Mental Paradigm

I use the term *mental paradigm* to describe an imaginary box within the mind, a box that houses what you believe to be the world of the possible. Conversely, everything that lies outside the perimeter of this box represents the world of the impossible to you. It's the combination of what lies both inside and outside of this imaginary box that forms what is commonly known as your "system of beliefs."

What determines on which side of the box's boundaries something lies are your experiences, your environment, your knowledge and wisdom—everything you've been exposed to throughout your life. To the extent your experiences have been positive and you possess sufficient knowledge and wisdom, not only will more possibilities lie inside the boundaries of your mental paradigm, but the paradigm itself will be expansive; i.e., your mind will be more open to new ideas, concepts, and possibilities. To the extent the opposite is true, you will tend to have a closed mind.

The more positive your system of beliefs, the more overall belief you will have in your ability to control your destiny. Likewise, the more you believe you have the power to control your destiny, the more expansive your mental paradigm will be; and the more expansive your mental paradigm, the less you are imprisoned by preconceived notions. What all this leads to is a "resourceful mind," a mind that is willing to consider virtually all possibilities.

# Mental Paradigm

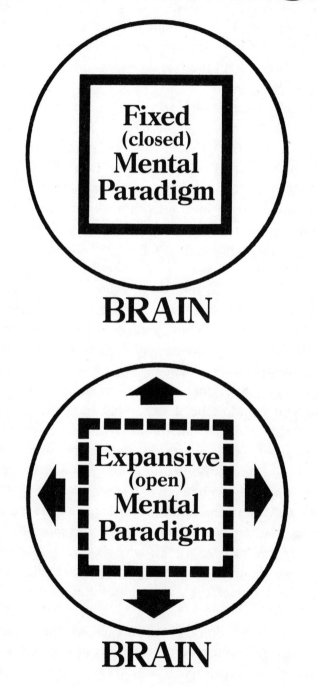

## Alternative Thinking

Resourcefulness is nothing more than alternative thinking. By *alternative thinking*, I mean following the habit of looking for other alternatives when confronted with problems or obstacles rather than dwelling on the fact that something didn't work out the way you had hoped.

This is really what PMA is all about, and it manifests itself in the form of an expansive mental paradigm. In fact, it would be appropriate to say that PMA and an expansive mental paradigm are synonymous. When your alternative-thinking mechanism is strong, it means your belief is strong, because it is this belief that stimulates you to look for other alternatives. And, once again, belief is in great measure a result of understanding that (1) problems are a normal, integral, and ongoing part of the living experience; (2) there's an offsetting positive to every negative occurrence; (3) the law of averages guarantees that if you just keep trying, sooner or later things will work out; and (4) through the power of the mind, you possess the capacity to draw to yourself the things, people, and circumstances necessary to achieve your objectives.

Did you ever experience the thrill of doing something that everyone said couldn't be done? What happened in such an instance is that you saw possibilities that others couldn't see, because your mental paradigm was more expansive than theirs. This made you more resourceful, more attuned to alternative ways to accomplish your objective. Rather than saying that when you were ready for it, the solution made its appearance, it might be more appropriate to explain it as *breaking through the existing boundaries of your mental paradigm and discovering that other alternatives lie outside.* In other words, you discovered possibilities that originated *beyond* the existing perimeter of your mental paradigm.

Further, since we don't know all the possibilities that exist outside of our mental paradigms, theoretically speaking our limitations are pretty much where *we* choose to place them. What an exciting thought! Talk about being able to write your own lifeticket, *this* is it.

## SWIMMING WITH THE TIDE

To tap this limitless reservoir of ideas and opportunities, it's important to understand that you may not always get a solution that allows you to achieve your original objective. Instead, you may find an alternative that takes you in an entirely different direction, but a direction that more often than not turns out to be superior to the one in which you were originally headed.

A great example of this is the story of a friend of mine who is a real estate broker in Austin, Texas. Austin is one of the cities that was hardest hit by the real estate bloodbath that began in the early 1980s and was particularly brutal in Texas. Instead of stubbornly resisting the obvious and overwhelming reversal of the Austin real estate market, my friend spotted opportunity in that city's real estate problems. For several years now, he's been operating seminars for the real estate nonprofessional, the person who's always dreamed of owning real estate but assumed it was only for sophisticated investors.

My friend teaches these people how to acquire real estate that has been repossessed by lenders, and, as a result, every lender in Austin puts out the welcome mat to him. He makes his profit by earning a commission on every piece of property his seminar attendees buy. At a time when most brokers and builders in Austin have been dying on the vine, my friend's business has grown by leaps and bounds. And, best of all, everyone is happy: The lenders get rid of unwanted, repossessed properties; the buyers end up owning property without having to go through years of trial and error on their own; and my friend is making a terrific income in real estate commissions.

Unlike thousands of his deluded peers who refused to come to grips with the realities of the Austin real estate crash, my friend employed the habit of alternative thinking and allowed it to take him in an entirely different direction—a direction that created a winning situation for everyone involved. His alternative thinking was nothing more than a simple mental adjustment to a negative situation, yet it's been the difference between his tremendous success and the hard times experienced by many real estate agents in Austin. No big secret, no great luck, no grand-slam home run. Just adherence to a simple habit that prompted him to take alternative action.

## ANYTHING BUT MY MERCEDES!

Now compare my friend's story to being down and out in Beverly Hills. I recall a Beverly Hills acquaintance many years ago lamenting about his financial problems, and my asking him why he didn't sell either his wife's or his Mercedes to ease his burden. Ouch! You would have thought I'd shot him through the heart: "Sell my Mercedes! Are you kidding? I couldn't do that."

"Why not?" I naïvely asked.

"I couldn't sell my Mercedes. What would people in Beverly Hills think? I'd be ruined."

Obviously, at that particular time selling one of his Mercedes was not part of this individual's world of the possible. It was a thought that lay outside the perimeter of his mental paradigm, and thus was not an alternative that his unresourceful state of mind would consider. Note that I said "at that particular time." The resourcefulness of most people tends to change with changing circumstances. For example, what if this same individual were to suddenly find himself in a Nazi concentration camp, and a guard said to him, "I'll tell you what. If you sell your two Mercedes, I'll get you out of here." Under those circumstances, his response might very well be, "Sell them? Are you kidding? You can *have* them!"

The point is that to achieve consistently positive results, you must unfailingly practice the habit of maintaining an expansive mental paradigm. If you wait until you're desperate before considering unconventional or extreme alternatives, that's probably how you'll live the remainder of your life—desperate.

# Unlimited Control?

Earlier I said that theoretically speaking, our limitations are pretty much where *we* choose to place them. I used the term *theoretically* because a positive mental attitude does not make you omnipotent. But to the extent the Attitude Habit becomes a way of life, one thing is certain: You can do everything *better*. Viktor Frankl's positive attitude didn't guarantee his survival in Auschwitz and Dachau, but it did guarantee that his odds would be much better than if his mind had been negative regarding the possibility of survival.

Put another way, though we are never free from the inevitabilities of life—illness, accidents, natural disasters, and the like—we *are* free to choose our attitude toward them. And in so doing, we can at a minimum swing the odds in our favor and dramatically increase our chances of success—which, of and by itself, is sufficient reason to work hard at nurturing the Attitude Habit every day of our lives.

# Chapter 3

# The Perspective Habit

It was exactly 8:10 P.M. on March 18 as Mexicana flight #913 touched down on the runway at the Manzanillo airport. I stared out the window into the darkness, wondering whether my decision to make Mexico my home for the next year had been impulsive. I had felt like this was the ideal time to get away, erase from memory the peoplewebs that clouded my once-clear mind, do some writing in peace and quiet, and reevaluate that unpredictable and mysterious experience called life.

My wife was almost six months pregnant, but I had rationalized that if there were any problems, we could always get to Guadalajara by air in less than a half hour. And, who knows, maybe the medical facilities in the Manzanillo area weren't quite as bad as people had led me to believe. In any event, the tentative plan was to come back to the United States after my wife reached her eighth month, have the baby, then return to Manzanillo to finish out the year.

Besides, for once in my life the timing was perfect. The right situation had presented itself at exactly the right time. About eight years earlier, a friend of mine had built a palatial, 25,000-square-foot villa on a mountaintop just above the Las Hadas Hotel, but his business activities had kept him from spending much time there in recent years. Anyone who has been an absentee homeowner in Mexico knows what that means—problems. So it was a genuine value-for-value situation: We struck a bargain whereby my wife and I agreed to live in the villa for about a year and watch over things, try to instill some esprit de corps in the villa's staff, and get the administration of the place under control. Seemed like a simple enough task. (If you've ever lived in Mexico, that last statement undoubtedly already has you smiling.)

To live in Mexico is like enrolling in Problem Solving 401. It's the ultimate test of one's ability to implement alternative thinking. During our first week at the villa, we experienced a few "minor inconveniences": The water throughout the villa turned dark brown; then, it went off completely for two days, which meant none of the toilets could be flushed; we found Incredible Hulk–sized rats in our kitchen, along with the expected economy-sized cockroaches, lizards, and assorted dinosaur bugs; the air-conditioning went off for several days, which made the solid concrete rooms feel like hermetically sealed tombs; and the telephone temporarily dropped dead two or three times. None of this may mean much to you if you have never lived in Mexico and tried to get a repairman to come out and fix something.

Our villa was on Manzanillo Bay, about fifteen miles from the city of Manzanillo. We were actually closer to a couple of small pueblos, Santiago and Salahua, than to Manzanillo. On our second day at the villa, we felt mentally prepared to take on Santiago and shop for groceries. Had someone told us in advance that Camacho's was the worst grocery store in Mexico, it still would have been a shock. That, however, was *not* what we had been told. We had been assured that Camacho's was by far the *best* market in the Manzanillo area. As I casually strolled into the store, I took one look and immediately began scouring my mind for an appropriate Henny Youngman one-liner. It was no use; Henny Youngman had never been to Camacho's.

The worst-stocked, shabbiest corner grocery store in any

ghetto in the United States would be a gourmet market in Santiago. The only place where I had seen less food on store shelves was in Leningrad, and the customers in Leningrad were somber. But in Camacho's, people actually were smiling. I figured there must be something I didn't understand, so I started smiling, too. I made up my mind then and there that it was going to be a long year, and that I had two choices: I could complain and suffer like a normal American, or I could adapt and get into the local people's way of life.

It wasn't long before I actually began to look forward to going to Camacho's a couple of times a week to shop and exchange "Spanglish" quips with Mr. Camacho and his employees. What a great occasion when the weekly issue of *USA Today* arrived or the store's refrigerator was fully loaded with a new shipment of Pepsi. It's all a matter of how you frame a situation in your mind.

After a couple of weeks of working hard to adapt to a radically new life-style, my wife and I settled down to a relaxed pace the likes of which I had never before experienced. We walked on the beach, read a lot, went to the Saturday open-air market in Santiago, fixed up the villa, and even ventured into the city of Manzanillo to shop. On balance, it was delightful, notwithstanding our paranoid concerns about irritable scorpions hiding under our covers, awaiting the arrival of our toes.

However, it was also taking a toll on my wife. For one thing, the villa was so big and had so many stairs that it was the equivalent of a hard workout just to get through a normal day. Also, the streets and roads in much of rural Mexico were not built with pregnant women in mind. The road up the mountain to our villa consisted primarily of jagged rock, and most of the several miles up or down the mountain had to be taken at speeds of no more than ten miles an hour. Even at that pace, you felt as if you were riding atop a wild bronco—in slow motion. The streets of Santiago were a mixture of large stones and dirt, and were even bumpier than our mountain road.

It was mid-April. The baby was not due until early July, but to be on the safe side I thought it would be a good idea to see what medical facilities existed in the area in the unlikely event an emergency should arise. We asked several people, both Americans and locals, about the childbirth facilities and medical treatment available in the area, and the consensus seemed to be, "No one has a baby in Manzanillo." There simply were no available medical facilities as we know them in the United States. The last-ditch hope in a true emergency, we were told, was the Naval Hospital in the small town of Las Brisas, about ten miles away.

The next Sunday we took a drive to check out the Naval Base facility in person. Again, culture shock. We didn't need to go inside. One look at the outside and you knew that no one with any serious medical problem gets out alive. The dilapidated building looked like something out of an old Bogart movie. My first words were, "Well, so much for emergencies in Manzanillo. No one has a baby here and lives to tell about it. At least we can totally eliminate this as an alternative, emergency or not." We laughed and joked about it as we pulled away in our old car, wondering how people survive in makeshift hospitals like this all over the world. Scary. Being an American has got to be the most sheltered, secure life on the planet.

As I lay in bed that night, staring at the ceiling, my thoughts kept coming back to what we had seen at the Naval Base. "Suppose . . . what if . . . no, unthinkable." I wouldn't even allow myself to consider the possibility. I simply couldn't let it happen, no matter what. I made up my mind that we had better plan to head for the States around the end of May, just to be on the safe side. Then, after all was well with the baby, we could return to Manzanillo around the third week of July.

I felt relieved at my decision, though my wife kept insisting that it really wasn't necessary to leave for the States so early. Unfortunately, her condition didn't give credence to her protests, because she gradually was experiencing more and more discomfort. Each trip up and down the bumpy mountain road seemed to be tempting the fates, until finally I made most of the treks into town alone in order to spare her the wear and tear. This created somewhat of a problem, because my wife spoke fluent Spanish, while I spoke practically none. Try that in the middle of Mexico if you want to find out what real insecurity is.

By the end of the first week in May, my wife's condition was deteriorating at an accelerating pace, and I seriously began to think in terms of emergencies. I decided that we had better get to Guadalajara within the next week in order to have her checked out at a good medical facility, then decide whether to come back to Manzanillo, stay in Guadalajara until the baby was born, or try to make it back to the United States. Unfortunately, Aeromexico had just gone broke, and that left only Mexicana Airlines' two flights a week to Guadalajara as our single source of air travel.

Worse, we were informed that international law would not permit a woman to fly if she was more than seven months pregnant. To top that off, all flights to Guadalajara were fully booked for weeks to come. It was getting to be a very unfunny situation. My anxiety heightened as I tried to assess our options rationally. I looked into renting a van and found that it would be a six-hour drive, assuming no problems en route (always a bad assumption in Mexico), and very uncomfortable in many stretches along the way. "Would she be able to make it?" I wondered to myself. I had no choice; I'd have to try. The vision of the so-called hospital in Las Brisas kept pushing me forward, forcing me to select from among the unpleasant alternatives available to us.

I reserved a van for Saturday, May 13, and began packing our necessities. In the meantime, I had the responsibility for making sure the staff was taking care of the villa, the payroll was being met, and the whole place wouldn't come apart at the seams as soon as we left. I had come to Mexico to relax and write; things were changing rapidly. What did I know from gardeners and housekeepers who didn't speak English? Worse, the air-conditioning had now stopped functioning altogether and needed to be completely overhauled or replaced. In addition, the water was periodically shutting off and the car was on the verge of breaking down.

My wife was in such pain by Wednesday afternoon that we decided to set up an appointment to see a doctor in Manzanillo on Thursday, just to make sure we weren't taking a life-and-death risk driving to Guadalajara on Saturday. Through a friend of ours, Captain Eugenio Gutigrez, we secured an appointment with Dr. Abrajan, who examined my wife on Thursday morning. Dr. Abrajan told us that my wife definitely would not carry the baby full term, but probably would not deliver for another month or so. He also diagnosed a huge, excruciatingly painful bulge in her upper-left abdomen as a hernia. Nevertheless, it was his opinion that we should be able to make it to Guadalajara by van, assuming my wife didn't get any worse by Saturday.

That evening, however, things did take a turn for the worse—much worse. As the night progressed, my wife began writhing in pain and screaming in anguish. This was a woman who never complained, and who had a very high threshold of pain. As she became more and more uncontrolled, reality began to set in. This was not a nightmare; it was not a movie; it was not something I was reading about in the newspaper. It was happening to *us*. The ultimate emergency that every civilized person has had nightmares about was here and now. Guadalajara was out. The only question was what was going to happen right here in Manzanillo!

I called Hans Rothlisberger, our best friend in Mexico, who was public relations director at the Las Hadas Hotel next door. He had been monitoring our situation closely for the past couple of weeks, so he was aware that things were not going well. When he heard my wife's screams in the background, he immediately set in motion a Mexican chain reaction by calling our mutual friend, Andy Shryer, who in turn called Captain Gutigrez, who in turn called the Red Cross and Dr. Abrajan. Within thirty minutes, the Red Cross arrived, carried my wife out on a shabby stretcher, and put her in an old truck-ambulance. We then started down the mountain over the bumpy, rocky road we had come to know so well. I sat next to my wife in the ambulance and held her hand tightly. Hans followed behind in his car as we made our way—at a pace of about two miles an hour—down the long mountain road, with my wife moaning in pain.

As the old ambulance bounced up and down unmercifully, the Red Cross doctor told my wife that it would be necessary to examine her on the way to the hospital. I watched his face closely as he proceeded with the examination, and immediately saw that something was wrong. He spoke to my wife in Spanish, and she relayed his words to me: "You're going to have this baby *tonight*."

"Impossible," I thought. "It can't be happening . . . not here . . . not in Manzanillo . . . not two months premature . . . not at the Naval Hospital." It was only a few weeks ago that we were laughing about how we could never consider the Naval Hospital as a viable alternative. Now I just wanted to awaken from my nightmare. I wanted to clamp magic wings on my wife and myself and zip off to Guadalajara where we would be safe from the unknown. Somehow . . . some way . . . I just couldn't allow it to happen. But the reality was that it *was* happening. One of those inevitabilities of life was upon us. We were headed toward the Naval Hospital, where the fate of my wife and unborn child would soon be decided.

As the ambulance ended its journey down the mountain road and settled onto the old highway en route to Las Brisas, all I could see through the dirty windshield was a kaleidoscope of darkness, beat-up cars, people occasionally darting across the road, and smoke from the day's burning of fields that had settled over the highway. The siren on our vehicle droned in my ears as I tried to picture the events that lay ahead.

When we finally arrived at the Naval Hospital, the staff immediately prepared my wife for delivery, then wheeled her into the labor room. I was not allowed to go into the room, and was told to stay behind a three-foot-high wall about a dozen steps from the labor room. In the sweltering humidity, I paced the floor for hours, grimacing at my wife's every moan and scream.

Throughout the night, my mind gyrated wildly in an attempt to project all possible scenarios. As I continued my automaton-like pacing, I reflexively swatted mosquitos and watched cockroaches scoot in front of me without so much as a pause.

"No one," I thought to myself, "knew so little about childbirth as I. What were the odds of a two-months-premature baby surviving under the *best* of circumstances?" I wondered. I had no idea. Even more important, "What were a premature baby's chances under the *worst* of circumstances?" Horrible thoughts continuously bombarded my mind, and my head pounded as my wife's screams became louder and more desperate.

Finally, at about 2:00 A.M., Dr. Abrajan came out of the labor room and approached me with a somber expression on his face. He said something in Spanish that I didn't understand, then motioned for me to get Hans, who had been sleeping in his car outside. As I rushed out to the car, I thought to myself, "The baby is dead. The baby died." I could only hope that my wife was all right. After I woke Hans, he and I hurried back inside where Dr. Abrajan began talking to him in Spanish. About a minute elapsed before Hans turned to me and explained, in a grim and sympathetic tone, that they had tried several times to get the baby out, but each time they had started to lose his heartbeat. The umbilical cord was apparently wrapped around his legs. There was only one hope: a Caesarian operation.

I grimaced and bit down hard on my bottom lip. This was no nightmare, and there were no fairytale wings with which to make a movie-ending escape to Guadalajara. Zero hour had arrived; the cataclysm was upon us! There would be no reprieve. I was handed a document to sign—written in Spanish, of course—and a pen. It's the moment every human being fears will arrive one day, a matter of life and death over which he has absolutely no control. The heat . . . the humidity . . . the mosquitos . . . the cockroaches . . . a dying baby who's never seen the world . . . a beloved wife screaming just a few feet away . . . a foreign-language document to be signed. There are situations in life where the choices ultimately come down to only one. In this case, the single choice was to sign the document.

As they wheeled my wife into the hall toward the operating room, she called to me in a barely audible tone, "I love you, Robert." Tears streamed down my face as I responded, in a badly cracked voice, "I love you, too, Ester." I watched as they rolled her down the hallway, thinking to myself that I might never again see alive the kindest, most sensitive, loving, compassionate human being I had ever known. The fate of the most important person in my life was now completely out of my hands, controlled by strangers in a Third World country. "How could I possibly have allowed us to get into this kind of situation?" I asked myself.

Two nurses who had been sleeping on cots jumped up and rushed into the operating room right behind my wife, then the doors closed behind them. The wait was on. I had almost two hours to replay three possible scenarios in my mind, all of them cataclysmic: My wife might live, and the baby die; my wife might die, and the baby live; or both my wife *and* the baby might die. I was reeling emotionally, still clinging to the hope that I would wake up and discover that none of this really was happening. One moment I would find myself trying to comprehend how I could possibly cope with the third and worst of all possible scenarios; the next moment my mind would completely quit on me, incapable of thinking the unthinkable.

The apocalypse continued: There was no general anesthetic available, and it took forty-five minutes of prying and sticking for the anesthesiologist to get the local anesthetic into my wife's spine. At one point she stopped breathing, but they were able to bring her back just in time. As she lay on the operating table, her insides exposed, she was able to witness the entire operation in the mirror above her. It was a tense, monumental struggle, but the doctor finally succeeded in pulling the baby from her with a force so great that it lifted her entire body off the table.

Finally, at 4:12 A.M., the doors to the operating room flung open, and out charged a young doctor, surgical mask covering his face, carrying the baby in a frayed towel-like cloth. He was moving fast as he went by me on the way to an antiquated incubator behind a glass divider wall. The baby wasn't crying, but he was breathing . . . barely. As the doctor tried to get the baby into the incubator, he accidentally knocked the lid off, and it fell directly onto the baby's face. Again I bit hard on my lower lip as I watched the scenario unfolding just a few feet away.

Unable to properly adjust the top of the incubator, the young doctor picked up the baby, carried him down a hallway, and took him into another room that housed several more empty incubators. In the meantime, a nurse came out of the operating room and assured me that my wife was going to be all right, so I hurriedly followed the young doctor. In the intensive care room, he began frantically working on the infant in an effort to keep him alive. It occurred to me that if the baby didn't make it, I might never know what he looked like, so when the doctor seemed to have things somewhat under control, I hesitatingly asked if it would be possible for me to see my infant son up close. Reluctantly, the doctor allowed me to take a quick look.

That moment will forever live in my memory. The poor little guy was struggling for every breath he could snatch, and barely had enough strength to eke out an occasional, almost inaudible cry. Nevertheless, premature and all, he was absolutely beautiful. Dr. Chagoya, the doctor who had rushed him out of the operating room, explained that the baby's respiratory system was poorly developed and that it would be a touch-and-go situation, particularly during the first twenty-four hours. Infection, pneumonia, heart failure—everything was a danger at this point. Crude as their equipment was, the medical staff got the baby hooked up to a respirator, inserted breathing tubes into his trachea, planted an intravenous feeding tube in his left arm, and began working on him methodically.

After Hans finally departed for the hotel, I continued to pace the sweltering, quiet corridors of the hospital . . . thinking . . . thinking . . . thinking. Hour after hour I paced, swatting the mosquitos that relentlessly stalked me. As my mind floated aimlessly, it kept coming back to two words, *perspective* and *relativity*. At a time like this, I thought to myself, how petty and inconsequential most of the day-to-day problems of life seem to be. All the little slights, the hurts, the injustices, the bad breaks, the financial losses we experience as we stumble through life in our waking state of dreams seem so unimportant when viewed in a relative light. When juxtaposed against the life or death of someone whom we dearly love, how absurd they seem.

Each time I passed the intensive care room, Dr. Chagoya was standing over my son, Andrew Troy, watching his every movement, adjusting the maze of tubes sticking out of him, massaging his hands and feet, administering oxygen to him intermittently, checking his heart rate and pulse, and, above all, never taking his eyes off him. Whenever Dr. Chagoya looked up and saw me, he spoke with his eyes. He is one of the most compassionate young men I have ever known, a man who really cares.

At about 8:00 A.M., another young doctor, Dr. Hector Americo, relieved Dr. Chagoya. I was concerned, but not for long. Dr. Americo, too, exhibited seemingly infinite compassion. Once when Andrew's heart stopped beating, Dr. Americo alertly sprang into action and quickly got it pumping again with rapid massaging. This remarkable young man stood by the baby's incubator for twenty-four hours without taking a single break— adjusting tubes, massaging, and always watching . . . watching . . . watching.

In the midst of a horrendously insecure situation, there was one thing about which I felt totally secure: What Mexican physicians lack in facilities, equipment, and technology, they more than make up for with compassion, care, and concern. It is impossible for me to describe the bond that I felt with these men. I was truly touched by their greatness as human beings. Many may have the intellect to practice medicine, but only a small percentage have the character to practice people-medicine. We were most fortunate to have on our side a number of these extraordinary people-medicine doctors, the finest I could ever hope to meet in my lifetime.

These marvelous, compassionate, caring doctors—together with a number of equally compassionate, caring nurses—painstakingly brought my wife and son back from the brink of death. What began as an ordeal of nightmarish proportions evolved into nothing short of a miracle. In less than a week, both my wife and the baby stabilized, and we were able to return to the villa together. On that fateful night a week earlier, we had left the villa as two; we easily could have returned as one; instead, we returned as three. That which almost ended our lives made us infinitely stronger, and certainly gave me a much healthier perspective of my own little world.

## Problems Relative to What?

My family's brush with disaster in Mexico was the most difficult course I have yet to take at the University of Life, and undoubtedly the most important. To say the least, it dramatically changed my perspective on life. Since Mexico, many things I once looked upon as serious problems have been relegated to minor status or, in many cases, no problem at all.

There is no question that the inability to view day-to-day problems in a relative light is a widespread human deficiency that can be the difference between success and failure. We all have problems, yes, but it's important to learn to keep from blowing them out of proportion. You'll find routine problems in your life to be much less burdensome if you can successfully cultivate the Perspective Habit. By *perspective,* I'm talking about the capacity to view things on their relative level of importance. To develop the Perspective Habit, you must first get in the habit of asking yourself, when confronted with negative situations, problems relative to *what?*

Once we escape the Age of Infinite Wisdom, experience teaches us how quickly yesterday's garbage can become today's dessert. Today we're passed over for a promotion, and think the world is coming to an end. Tomorrow we lose our job, and a promotion is no longer important to us; we just yearn to have our job back. Then we lose our health, and suddenly we realize how good we had it when our only problem was not having a job. Truly, all problems are relative.

In this regard, financial problems usually are at the top of most people's lists. Most of us have difficulty grasping the reality that no matter how bad our financial problems may be, no one is going to drag us outside, put us against a wall, and machine-gun us to death. Don't get me wrong. I don't mean to imply that financial problems can't be serious, and I certainly know, as evidenced by my family's saga in Mexico, that from time to time each of us does come face to face with perilously real problems. But what I am suggesting is that rather than magnify daily problems, people would be much ahead of the game if they would use the relatively small number of genuinely serious problems they have to keep run-of-the-mill problems in proper perspective.

## The Catastrophe Illusion

As I pointed out earlier, it's important to come to grips with the reality that problems are an integral, ongoing part of the living experience. Life is a never-ending stream of hardships, obstacles, rejection, frustration, and so-called bad luck. Life is lost jobs, loans that aren't granted, sales that don't close, people who treat us unfairly, and deals that fall through at the last minute. None of these are fatal; they're just life.

It's absolutely essential that a person grasp this reality if he is to develop the Perspective Habit. Likewise, it's essential to absorb the truth contained in the Natural Law of Balance, as discussed in Chapter 2. If you believe there is an offsetting positive to every negative occurrence—which there is—you should make it a high priority to cultivate the habit of quickly and automatically maximizing the positives in every negative situation.

Actually, all four of the realities I discussed in the previous chapter as the foundation for developing and maintaining a strong PMA are equally important to maintaining a healthy perspective. (To refresh your memory, the four realities are: [1] problems are a normal, integral, and ongoing part of the living experience; [2] there's an offsetting positive to every negative occurrence [the Natural Law of Balance]; [3] the law of averages guarantees that if you just keep trying, sooner or later things will work out; and [4] through the power of the mind, a person possesses the capacity to draw to himself the things, people, and circumstances necessary to achieve his objectives.) Again, understanding these four realities is what gives you the belief necessary to maintain a true positive mental attitude, and PMA is an essential catalyst for breeding and practicing the Perspective Habit.

## The Great Illusion Called Misfortune

It is also important to understand that the offsetting positives to a negative situation not only can be subtle in nature (i.e., the association to the original negative may not always be apparent), they also may not appear until a much later date, or they may appear in small increments over a long period of time.

Put another way, misfortune and setbacks are often, if not always, nothing more than illusions, because we fail to connect the long-term benefits to the negative occurrence. To demonstrate the subtle, long-term, offsetting payoff that can be traced back to a seeming disaster, I'm reminded of a story that a now deceased friend of mine once told me. He said that in the 1930s Depression, he lost his house when he couldn't keep up his mortgage payments to the bank. Because of that traumatic experience, he vowed that he would never again borrow money, and he conducted both his business and personal affairs within the framework of that policy throughout the remaining fifty years of his life.

He ultimately accumulated a net worth of $500 million and attributed much of his success to his financial staying power during bad times. With his large cash reserves, he was able to buy everything from land to precious metals at depressed prices, then hold on for the long-term payoff. He paid cash for everything he bought—from cars to homes, from office equipment to entire companies—never owing a penny to anyone. As a result, he was able to weather numerous recessions completely unscathed.

By contrast, consider how millions of people have reacted to foreclosures on their properties. You see them on television all the time. The major networks love to parade irate farmers in front of the cameras, who see foreclosure as the end of the world and are intent not on maximizing the positives in their negative situations, but on expending their energies on bitterness and blaming their problems on government policies. Though I have compassion for such people, their lack of perspective blinds them to solutions and the offsetting benefits of their dilemmas. The difference between these people and my friend is that he used what he had learned from a seemingly catastrophic situation to lay the groundwork for a tremendous personal fortune.

Ever since my friend pointed out to me the subtle connection between his long-term megasuccess and a one-time catastrophe in his life, I've made it a point to observe closely many other heavyweight successes to see if I can spot a trend. I have. In fact, it's much more than a trend. *Every* successful person keeps his problems in proper perspective and makes it a habit to search immediately for the offsetting positives in every negative situation. The truly successful individual demonstrates the Perspective Habit by seeing adversity as both a learning experience and masked opportunity.

## High Stakes

To come out ahead in situations in which a great deal is at stake and emotions are running high, the skilled negotiator, like the skilled card player, is adept at knowing when to discard. And to be good at the art of knowing when to discard, you must maintain a healthy perspective so you can intellectually and emotionally understand that no deal is a life-and-death matter. With such a perspective as a backdrop, it's then much easier to lay down "either-or" ultimatums.

In other words, by keeping money situations in proper perspective, you're able to objectively set limits in advance, then stick by them. Your perspective should always be that the best deal in the world comes along every day. If you aren't able to cultivate this kind of perspective, the likely result is that you'll yield points or dollars to the other side as the negotiating heats up. This sets the stage for an atmosphere somewhat analogous to blackmail; i.e., much like the problem of overestimating what you bring to the negotiating table, the more the other side sees you giving in, the more he assumes you will *continue* to give in. And once the ball starts moving in that direction, it's extremely difficult to slow its momentum.

To lessen your chances of getting caught in this trap, the first step is to keep money in proper perspective. Making money is important, and making deals is a way of making money; therefore, one is justified in concluding that closing deals is important. Nevertheless, money's importance is relative. To the extent you fail to see financial situations in a relative light, you're likely to press. And the more you press, the less likely you are to come out ahead. When you begin to feel as if emotion is overtaking you in a negotiating situation, get into the habit of stepping back and, first of all, reminding yourself that your life isn't at stake on the outcome. Second, practice the habit of reevaluating the facts, and make certain that you aren't allowing a lack of perspective to take you beyond the bounds of prudent action.

## How's Your Blood Pressure?

When it gets down to it, I think one of the main reasons we have such difficulty seeing our everyday problems in a relative light is that we take ourselves too seriously. There is a fine line between pathos and humor, and one of the many advantages that a human being has over other species is that he possesses the capacity to detach himself both from situations and from his own self. One of the unique ways in which he is able to accomplish this is through the use of humor. Man is the only "animal" who can laugh at himself. He can *choose* not to see every problem, every unfair act, and every negative situation as monumental in importance.

For example, everyone knows what it feels like to be wrongly accused or slandered. Sometimes it's enough to make you want to stop people on the street and force them to listen to your tale of woe: "Justice must be done at any cost! The accusations are false, I tell you! The world is unfair!" Alas, though, no one cares. We get so caught up in our hurt, so upset over being wronged, that it can be very difficult for us to look beyond our fragile, injured egos and put seemingly unfair situations in proper perspective. Nonetheless, it's important to make it a habit to cut through your emotional gridlock, step back, and see the perceived wrong in relative terms. When you do so, you'll find it absolutely amazing what it can do for your results, efficiency, quality of life, self-esteem, and longevity, among other things.

It's pretty widely accepted in the medical professional that it's not stress that kills us, but how we react to it. Man has the capacity intellectually and emotionally to grasp the reality that life is imperfect. To the extent one succeeds in embracing this reality, he becomes known as an imperturbable person. Have you ever known someone who's imperturbable—blood pressure about 22 over 8? It can be maddening to deal with such people, can't it? But the rewards to the imperturbable person can be enormous, because he holds a tremendous advantage over those who are fast on the emotional trigger. The more distraught you allow yourself to become, the more energy you waste and the less likely you are to make sound decisions that lead to positive results.

Perhaps worst of all, the individual who doesn't develop the habit of maintaining his composure through a healthy perspective also runs the risk of losing the confidence of others—first, because it weakens his posture; second, because he makes obvious errors in judgment.

## So What?

Perhaps the most important point to draw from this chapter is that life's endless problems and seeming injustices do not prevent a person from achieving his objectives. Thankfully, your success is very much dependent upon your ability to cope with problems—to maximize the positives in negative situations—and one of the best catalysts for accomplishing this is to learn to keep things in proper perspective.

Give this some serious thought the next time you feel as though you are the victim of some terrible injustice, like being bumped from a flight on which you've had a confirmed reservation for a month. Embrace the habit of repeatedly asking yourself the tough, rational-perspective question: *So What?*

"But there's no other flight out tonight?"

"So what?"

"But I'll have to take a morning flight, and I'll be an hour late for my meeting."

"So what?"

"But it may blow the deal."

"So what?"

Save your serious concerns for genuinely serious situations—for when you have a real problem to deal with, such as the Mexico experience I described at the outset of this chapter. Mastering the Perspective Habit allows you to see your day-to-day problems—especially all the petty injustices you feel have been done to you—in a more relative light. It's time well invested to work hard at cultivating the Perspective Habit, because it will pay enormous dividends to you throughout life.

The next time you find yourself acting as though the world is coming to an end, remember that only one time in history is such an event going to take place, and I have news for you: You won't be around to remember it happening anyway!

Do yourself a favor. Get into the Perspective Habit . . . and . . . take it eeeazzeee.

# Chapter 4

# The Present Living Habit

I was taking a late afternoon stroll on Ocean Avenue, sorting my thoughts and occasionally checking the progress of the slowly sinking sun. I don't remember exactly how it happened, but through a quirk of fate I found myself engaged in conversation with a complete stranger, which is quite out of character for me.

For whatever reason—possibly nothing more than coincidence—we seemed to have a common communication channel that was instantly recognizable to both of us. I had noticed Dan pacing above the cliffs a couple of days before, obviously deep in thought, just as he was today. As the conversation unfolded, he said to me, "You know, I've been searching for a long time for a feeling I experienced many years ago. I was a whiz-kid stockbroker, on top of the world financially, until my early thirties. Then, one day, I suddenly realized I wasn't happy. To the disbelief of my colleagues, I just up and quit."

"Did you know what you wanted to do when you quit? Did you have another business in mind?" I asked.

"I really had no idea what I wanted to do. All I was sure of was that I was sick of the proverbial rat race, sick of the money worshiping, sick of the win-at-all-costs mentality of the people I worked with day in and day out—sick of the world as I knew it at the time. I just wanted to get as far away from the money jungle as possible and have the opportunity to reflect on life.

"I bought a quaint, aging little house in a modest neighborhood, packed away my suits, dress shirts, and ties, and bought several pairs of overalls. At first, I spent most of my time fixing up the house and just treating my mind to some long-overdue relaxation. Then, after a while, I started making stained-glass windows in my garage and selling them to people in the neighborhood. I had never enjoyed anything so much in my life. I sometimes found myself chuckling about the drastic change in my life-style. It was hard to believe—me, the hotshot wonderboy of the brokerage business, wearing overalls, working with my hands, and making stained-glass windows."

"Is that what you miss now—making stained-glass windows?" I inquired with a growing fascination about Dan's background.

"It was much more specific than that—the point in time, that is. I had finished my work for the day, and was sitting on the front steps of my house in the late afternoon. It was spring, and there was a warm breeze coming in off the ocean. I can't adequately describe what I felt, except that my mind was completely relaxed—the only time in my life I could remember that happening to me. Then, suddenly . . . it's hard to put into words . . . I experienced this feeling of contentment taking over my entire body, a sensation of total joy. I was conscious of wanting to freeze that moment in time and live in that contented state for eternity."

The soft smile on his face slowly faded as he looked out toward the ocean and continued. "For fifteen years I've been searching . . . hoping to recapture that feeling of ecstasy . . . looking everywhere for it . . . believing it's out there somewhere . . . but no matter how hard I try, it always seems beyond my reach . . . beyond . . ." At that point, his voice tailed off to a barely audible whisper.

Dan had described his journey through adulthood so well, distilled the essence of his life in such sensory detail, that I felt as though I had experienced it firsthand with him. Though I was somewhat hesitant of causing him any undue anguish, I quietly pressed on with my inquiry. "What do you think it was? Why do you think you've never been able to recapture that unique feeling of contentment and joy?"

"You know, it's funny. It's so obvious now, but at the time I didn't see it coming. Little by little, working away by myself in my garage, the demand for my stained-glass windows increased, until finally I had to hire an assistant. Success led to more success, until I found myself with a number of employees on the payroll and had to move my business to a commercial building. I didn't realize what I had lost until it was too late. It's as though I had awakened from a dream and found myself reviewing projections, holding production meetings, making sales calls—right back on the battlefield again. All I had done was switch to another league. Everything else—the people, the problems, the aggravation—was pretty much the same."

Never had a chance meeting with a stranger made such an impact on my thinking, though I finally concluded that Dan's situation wasn't unique. As most people do at one time or another, I think Dan was pondering what Albert Camus once described: "There is but one truly serious problem, and that is . . . judging whether life is or is not worth living."

## Meaninglessness

Based on his narration, my feeling is that Dan missed the moral of his own story. He had been searching for years for the bliss he had felt at that magical moment on his front steps, yet the events leading up to that moment indicated no conscious search for it on his part. Rather, he just seemed to be naturally relaxed and enjoying his work. It sounded as though he had experienced Aristotle's description of happiness as a condition rather than a destination.

Viktor Frankl describes this phenomenon as the concept of "paradoxical intention," whereby he contends that the more we make something a target, the more likely we are to miss it. As Frankl explains, "Happiness . . . cannot be pursued. . . . [T]he more we aim at happiness, the more we miss our aim." If there is a reason for happiness, happiness ensues. It is a side effect of having a purpose, a meaning to life.

That, I believe, is the real key to what Dan had experienced but could never seem to get back to. His happiness had ensued as a side effect of his living the kind of life he enjoyed. The temptation is to believe that he was happy because he had rid himself of his drive to succeed, but I don't believe that was the case at all. I think without being consciously aware of it, what Dan had found after leaving the brokerage business was a meaning to his life. For the first time, he was doing what he wanted to do, what he enjoyed doing, and what he obviously was good at. Then, again without realizing it was happening, he allowed events to take control of his life. Since then, he has been pursuing something that was nothing more than a by-product of his previously meaningful life. For fifteen years now, instead of focusing on reclaiming the meaning, he has been focused on pursuing happiness.

Again, Frankl gives us some insight when he states, in *Man's Search for Meaning*, "What man needs is not a tensionless state, but rather the striving and struggling of some goal worthy of him." I fully agree with Frankl's belief that man's real purpose is not to achieve goals, but to constantly *strive toward them.*

Dr. Frankl's work in this area spans more than half a century. As early as the 1950s he referred to meaninglessness as "the mass neurosis of our time" and correctly predicted a dramatic increase in the problem. Since the turbulent sixties, young people have been lunging in every direction in search of a cause. I remember one young lady in my employ telling me that she and her husband had been professional campus protesters when they were in college. Of and by itself, that was not earth-shaking news. What was fascinating, however, was her recalling that on several occasions, in the midst of raucous, sometimes violent, campus demonstrations, she had asked her husband, "Now, tell me again, why are we doing this?" or "What's this protest about?" Like Eric Hoffer's true believers, they were desperately looking for a reason to crusade, for something to believe in.

In my view, much of the youth revolt of the past three decades has been the result of a lack of purpose in the lives of young people. Over and over we see this meaninglessness leading to depression, and depression leading to suicide. Regardless of whether protest marches have to do with eradicating poverty or saving whales from extinction, the reality is that they do not fill the void inherent in a meaningless life. Consider that if man were to succeed in ridding the world of all disease, poverty, pestilence, famine, and war, what then would be the purpose of his existence?

The reality is that as the struggle for day-to-day survival has increasingly subsided, an important question has emerged: survival for *what?* In other words, just having the means to live is not enough; a person must have something to live *for.* If there is no purpose to an individual's life—no meaning—then there's no reason to get out of bed in the morning, no reason even to be alive. In the words of the great Albert Einstein, "The man who regards his life as meaningless is not merely unhappy but hardly fit for life."

The term *meaning to life* can be defined in a variety of ways by different people. For purposes of this book, however, I am referring only to meaning that has to do with career or occupational goals and normal, day-to-day living. I am not addressing spiritual meaning, i.e., meaning that has to do with the ultimate purpose of life, a higher meaning than our life here on earth.

Again, paraphrasing Robert DeRopp's words in his book *The Master Game,* seek, above all, for a game worth playing. Having found the game, play it with intensity. Play as if your life and sanity depended on it. Because they do!

## The Fantasy That Never Arrives

The more I reflect on the question, and the more I draw from my own experience and the experiences of others, the more convinced I am that striving toward goals is not a means to an end; striving is an end in itself. Those who wish their lives away in anticipation of achieving some long-awaited goal do themselves a grave disservice. Often, it isn't even a specific goal they are seeking. Instead, they embody the future in the shadowy allure of some undefinable promised land down the road. Promised lands, however, are hard to come by.

Perhaps you've read the fascinating essay "The Station," in which the author metaphorically describes all of us as being on a mythical train of life, rolling relentlessly down the tracks toward the future. As we travel on this train of life, we keep believing that just around the next bend we're going to arrive at the Station, a beautiful little red station house that will signify the panacea moment when all the pieces of our lives will fit together like completed jigsaw puzzles. When we arrive at the Station, there will be a big crowd cheering, flags will be waving, bands will be playing, and that's when all our goals will be achieved and all our desires will be fulfilled.

Unfortunately, there's one serious problem with all this: It's a fantasy—a pure fantasy—because *there is no station*. It doesn't exist. And if there is no station, you better enjoy the trip down the tracks! The truth is that *the* moment never quite arrives. There's always one more deal to close, one more goal to achieve, one more hill to climb—and that's why you have to live in the present. The best day really is today. Forget about today being the first day of the rest of your life. Today could be the *last* day of the rest of your life. Remember, you cannot change the inevitable, but you *can* change your attitude toward today. It *is* within your power to cultivate the habit of living in the present.

Voltaire gave us wise advice when he cautioned, "Do not anxiously expect what has not yet come. Do not vainly regret what has already passed." An unknown author put it much more simply when he said, "Yesterday is a cancelled check; tomorrow is a promissory note; but *today* is cash!"

No one ever said on his deathbed, "Gee, I wish I had spent more time thinking about the future." The future doesn't need your attention. It has an annoying habit of arriving ahead of schedule—without your help. Even if you have goals, day-to-day life has little meaning if your main reason for living is to look forward to the day when those goals are achieved. It's possible to achieve all your goals in life but still miss out on life itself. To live in the present, one must have a meaning to one's daily life.

This thought struck me back in 1980 when I was watching a television interview with Chuck Noll, coach of the Pittsburgh Steelers, after his team had won an unprecedented fourth Super Bowl. The interviewer, undoubtedly expecting a classic jock reply, must have been quite surprised when Noll said, "You know, I really don't get that excited about winning the Super Bowl. What excites me is working *toward* the Super Bowl—the daily practices, teaching the intricacies of blocking and tackling, the day-to-day camaraderie among the players—but the Super Bowl itself is sort of anticlimactic."

What Chuck Noll clearly was saying was that he lives *every day*, not just for the future attainment of a Super Bowl victory. It reminded me of Andy Rooney's advice about learning to enjoy the little things in life, because the big ones don't come around very often. A player may play in a Super Bowl once or twice in his career if he's lucky, and most never play in any Super Bowl at all. But a player has to practice *every day*.

## Present Living Questions

Over a period of many years I have constructed a list of simple questions that I believe must be answered by anyone who is serious about fostering the Present Living Habit. Your answers to these five questions are critical to your ability to live in the present, as well as to your chances of achieving long-term, positive results, so I urge you to give them a lot of thought before attempting to set specific goals. Otherwise, you may wake up one day and realize that you've wasted many years of your life trying to achieve goals that weren't in harmony with who and what you really are. As someone once said, many a man gets to the top of the ladder only to find that it's been leaning against the wrong wall.

## Question No. 1: What Do I Enjoy?

To develop the Present Living Habit and avoid the temptation to wish away precious time in anticipation of the day when a particular goal is achieved requires first the capacity to enjoy the struggle along the way. In other words, striving must be an end in itself.

One of the sad realities of our world is that most people are unhappy in their work. How many happy stewardesses, waiters, bank tellers, or postal workers do you meet in a week's time? To listen to people talk, it seems as though they believe that if they could just make more money, they would enjoy their work. But I think it's the other way around: If they enjoyed their work more, they probably would make more money. It's very easy to fool yourself on this one. If you get all steamed up and say to yourself, "Okay, I'm really going to get enthusiastic about my work, because I want to see if it produces financial results," it probably won't. You have to enjoy your work naturally; work must be an end in itself. As with happiness, the more you make money your aim, the less likely you are to hit your target.

The secret is to figure out what you really enjoy doing, without regard to the potential financial rewards. No one can predict what the financial rewards ultimately might be if you possess a great enough love for your work. Can you imagine Walt Disney trying to convince bankers that he could build an empire based on a mouse? Or how about Ray Kroc? To most people, a hamburger stand is a hamburger stand, but to Kroc it was a passion that evolved into a multibillion-dollar hamburger-stand empire—McDonald's.

Charles A. Garfield, president of Peak Performance Center in Berkeley, California, has studied successful people for many years in an attempt to identify common characteristics of high achievers. One of the more interesting things he has found is that supersuccessful people avoid falling into the "comfort zone," a term he coined to describe that no-man's land where a person begins to feel too much at home after experiencing a little success. I'm convinced that it's the joy of work—loving what one does for a living—that makes it not only possible to avoid the comfort zone, but easy. What else keeps people like Bob Hope, George Burns, Armand Hammer, and other elderly successes driving themselves relentlessly day after day? Such people, who are well into their eighties and nineties, have found "a game worth playing"—a game they *enjoy*. Remember, it's not chronology that is the essence of life; it's aliveness. To paraphrase George Burns, *getting* older may be inevitable, but *being* old isn't.

I recently read a fascinating article about Edward DeBartolo, the eighty-year-old shopping-center magnate from Youngstown, Ohio. The article stated that DeBartolo's net worth has been estimated at $900 million—which surprised me, because someone had once offered to sell me *all* of Youngstown, Ohio, for $87,000. (I countered with $77,500, but my bid was rejected.)

According to the article, DeBartolo works seven days a week, getting to work every morning at 5:00 A.M. Can you imagine going to work every morning and the only form of life you see is chickens? But that was mild compared to this: Edward DeBartolo claims he has never taken a vacation! I happened to mention this to one of my children who was still languishing in the Age of Infinite Wisdom, and he replied, "What's the sense of having $900 million if you can't enjoy it?" To which I responded, "Who said Mr. DeBartolo doesn't enjoy it? Maybe he's on vacation seven days a week; maybe he just loves what he's doing."

Clearly, it's not the goals they reach or the amount of money they accumulate that makes financial heavyweights like Edward DeBartolo continue to play every point as though it were match point. It's the *game* that's important to them; it's the *game* that makes life worth living. The game is here and now; it's the present; it gives life its meaning. The real challenge is to find the *right* game, the game worth playing. And of utmost importance in finding a game worth playing is to find a game you enjoy.

Which leads to the next question:

## Question No. 2: What Am I Good At?

The nice thing about this question is that the answer to it is often the very thing that you most enjoy. We're continually told about studies that show that the average person uses only a small percentage of his potential. I believe that at least one of the reasons for this is that most people do not exploit their best talents. You have to have a clear understanding of both your abilities and deficiencies in order to determine how to make the most of your natural resources.

In this regard, it's important to understand that it's not what you *have* or what you *do*, but what you *do* with what you *have*. I certainly could never run the 100-yard dash in ten seconds flat, no matter how much I practiced, but that doesn't prevent me from succeeding in other fields of endeavor where I'm much better qualified. However, if I delude myself about my abilities, I'm destined to fail. Wouldn't most of us love to be Joe Montana? But just because we would enjoy being a superstar pro quarterback doesn't mean we have the ability to be one. What I'm talking about here is maximizing your talents and efficiently using your natural resources. You have to analyze your skills with complete objectivity, which requires that you be neither modest nor egotistical. Are you creative? athletic? artistic? Do you like people? Are you good with numbers? Do you thrive on being organized? Are you an effective motivator? Are you skilled at orchestrating a project or better at following through on the details? The list of questions is as long as you want to make it, and you can't make it too long.

### MANNEQUIN ATROCITIES

In my early twenties—are you ready for this?—I spent two years in dental school, though I was never quite sure why I was there.

I had given no thought whatsoever to my skills, ignoring the fact that kids used to call me Superclaw in art class in high school.

In dental school, you work on artificial mouths mounted on metal poles—sort of like stripped-down mannequins. Things got so bad that I became the only dental student in history to make a mannequin scream. I'll never forget the day I finally quit dental school, because as I walked out the laboratory door for the last time I could hear all the mannequins in the laboratory cheering in unison. Talk about getting no respect.

My point is that people often stumble or get trapped into careers without giving much thought to their talents, without even considering the possibility that they may be exploiting only a small percentage of their potential in their present occupation. I sometimes think that we're just too close to ourselves to see the obvious. Because it's so easy to miss your own talents, be sure to give this one a lot of attention and think objectively about your greatest strengths. The chances are overwhelming that efficient utilization of those strengths will also give you the most enjoyment, which in turn will save you from being obsessed with making money. The money will come, but you won't have to think about it; you'll be too busy enjoying your work and living in the present.

## Question No. 3: What Do I Want Out of Life?

When I refer to the question "What do I want out of life?" I'm not referring to specific goals. Goal setting is important, not only to assure that you keep moving forward, but also as a means of checking your progress. However, it's only after you've determined the answers to the five Present Living Questions that you're in a position to set specific goals.

Beware the Mad-Hatter Syndrome: So many people seem to be in such a terrible hurry to get somewhere in life, but when you talk to them it's obvious that they don't have the vaguest notion where they're going. It's as though they believe that expending energy is a satisfactory substitute for reason. As my friend Zig Ziglar cautions, you have to be careful not to become a "wandering generality"; you must strive to become a "meaningful specific." How can you draw to yourself the things, people, and circumstances needed to transform your desires into physical realities if you don't know what it is that you're after?

What I'm referring to here is a general concept of what you want out of life, a kind of overall objective that becomes your foundation for the ongoing process of setting specific goals. Take the life of Will Durant, for example. Durant spent more than seventy years traveling the world and studying the history of civilizations to write his eleven-volume series on that subject. Each of the massive volumes that Durant wrote undoubtedly served as goals or benchmarks along the way, and he probably achieved thousands of subgoals within each volume. However, his day-to-day study of civilizations most certainly had to be an end in itself, the activity that gave purpose and meaning to his life. In other words, his study of civilizations and his daily writing about them undoubtedly gave him a feeling of immense, continual fulfillment. The feeling of accomplishment he experienced when he finished his final volume after seventy years of work must have paled by comparison.

The reason the first Present Living Question (What do I enjoy?) is so important is that the person who claims to want something, but doesn't know why he wants it, is most probably headed in the wrong direction. It's very important to know *why* you want something, because it's the *why* that gives you the desire needed to persevere during tough times. And regardless of your occupation, you *will* experience tough times. In addition, you should be able to verbalize your purpose—quickly, simply, and precisely. If you can't, the chances are good that you aren't really serious about it.

Unfortunately, I think the main objective of most people, consciously or unconsciously, is to make a lot of money (whatever that's supposed to mean). A majority of people cling to the notion that making a lot of money would make them happy. Sadly, however, they delude themselves. The will to money is just another form of the will to power, and the will to power always brings about self-destruction. Much like sexual overactivity, it is really nothing more than an escape. The more a person seeks sexual pleasure just for the sake of proving his sexuality, the more he fails to find pleasure and the more miserable he is. Again, the same is true when money becomes an end in itself. Instead of possessing money, what happens when an individual's goal is money is that he becomes possessed *by* money. Instead of keeping money in perspective, it becomes an obsession. I don't think it's possible for someone to embrace the Present Living Habit if his goal is money.

I believe that what each of us really wants is happiness, and to the extent we aspire to riches, it's only because we erroneously believe that money will make us happy. Remember, happiness is a *by-product* of a meaningful life. And, as so many frustrated people have found out, making money, of and by itself, does not make for a meaningful life. That is not to say that you can't be happy with money, and it's not to say that money can't buy you many things that can make your life more pleasant. But, like happiness, money must be a side effect of a higher purpose.

Further, you must stay focused on your main purpose or you can inadvertently dissipate valuable energy by trying to grab all the candy in the store. Diluting your focus is a common mistake, and in this regard we would all be wise to heed General Patton's emphasis on the importance of singleness of purpose. I've seen this mistake made again and again, including by yours truly. Ironically, one of the things that causes a person to lose his focus is success itself. Making large sums of money can disorient you if you don't keep reminding yourself what your chief aim in life is. The problem, I believe, stems from money's tendency to give us a false sense of omnipotence.

Richard Bach makes this point poetically in *The Bridge Across Forever* when he warns, "To be handed a lot of money is to be handed a glass sword, blade-first. Best handle it very carefully, sir, very slowly while you puzzle what it's for."

## THE PUBLISHING ASYLUM

In 1980, having authored three best-selling books, I became restless and started looking for a side occupation. (Note: The most successful people in history rarely, if ever, have had side occupations. Hobbies, yes, but not occupations. Laserlike focus is perhaps the most common trademark of the supersuccessful.) I rationalized that since I had published the hardcover editions of my own books and successfully marketed them, it would make sense to publish other authors' books, too. In retrospect, I can say unequivocally that my only reason for undertaking a book-publishing venture was to make money.

I had the misfortune of striking it rich on the very first book I published, which is analogous to going to Las Vegas for the first time and coming away a winner. The book was a doom-and-gloom treatise on investing called *Crisis Investing*, which had already been published by a small publisher and had apparently peaked out at about 10,000 copies. I felt the book had some merit, and considering the state of the economy, along with the always destructive actions of the U.S. Congress, it seemed a perfect time to capitalize on the public's concerns.

The problem, however, was trying to convince the hardcover publisher who had distributed my own books to promote *Crisis Investing* to its bookstore accounts. At my urging, the vice president with whom I worked at that company read the book, after which he offered the opinion that it was a piece of [expletive]. He then had his sales force review the book, and told me that the prevailing opinion was that we would be lucky to sell 5,000 copies without a big marketing push, perhaps 25,000 copies with a "super-duper Ringer ad campaign."

Notwithstanding all this negativism, I managed to prevail, and succeeded in getting the book distributed nationwide. I wrote the copy for an ad campaign, and, to everyone's amazement, sales of the book went through the ceiling. Even more amazing, *Crisis Investing* ultimately enjoyed a string of fifteen consecutive weeks in the number-one position on the *New York*

*Times* best-seller list and became the biggest-selling hardcover book of 1980.

It was wildly exciting at first, but when I started to comprehend what it all meant, it made me feel a bit uneasy. Something just didn't seem right. As I've said many times over the years, in retrospect I wish I had failed with that first book, because that would have ended my foray into the publishing world.

Instead, I forged ahead with a number of other books, marketing them in the same sensationalistic style I had used to promote *Crisis Investing*. To my astonishment, less than nine months after publishing *Crisis Investing*, the *Wall Street Journal* ran a front-page story on my publishing exploits, and *Fortune* soon countered with a three-page article, noting that I had managed to put three books on the *New York Times* best-seller list after less than a year in business. I vividly recall feeling genuinely embarrassed when I read the articles, and I assure you it had nothing to do with modesty. Rather, it was because I knew in my heart that the articles were premature. **Real-World Rule No. 87: No matter how great others tell you you are, if you don't feel good about what you're doing, ignore the applause, stop, and carefully evaluate the facts.**

The truth of the matter was that I knew all along—at least subconsciously—what was wrong. I not only was publishing many books I didn't believe in, I also was saying things in my ads that were beyond the bounds of acceptable marketing hype. Talk about not being able to look in the mirror, I had to shave in a dark closet. I was guilty of self-delusion as a result of fearing the truth—an easy trap to fall into when you start seeing money as an end in itself.

The one good thing that came out of all this was that it gave me a firsthand appreciation of what conventional publishers have to put up with in dealing with authors. They are constantly being chastised for being insensitive and callous toward no-name authors, especially first-time authors. However, based on my experience from inside the Publishing Asylum, I can tell you that there most decidedly are two sides to the story. If man does, indeed, walk around in a state of waking dreams, a large percentage of would-be authors float around in a self-hypnotic state of delusion that defies description. The one thing that most unpublished authors have in common is that each of them seems absolutely certain that he's written the sequel to *Gone with the Wind*—or at least *Think and Grow Rich*—and makes demands accordingly.

On more than one occasion I was tempted to laugh out loud when dealing with some of these "authors," but would quickly remind myself that the author with whom I was speaking might well be dangerous. Who knew what these people were capable of when they were running around loose on the streets? It got to a point where my staff and I would spend a large percentage of our time discussing strategies to humor our most deranged authors. When I finally extricated myself from the publishing business, I could have written a great movie script based on my zany experiences. I can see myself now, accepting an Oscar for *Psycho Author*.

The moral? I didn't have a good *reason* for going into the publishing business. Certainly I didn't enjoy it, and, other than writing good ad copy, I had no particular skills for running a publishing company. The best guide to a proper focus is to think about what would bring happiness to your daily life. What is it that you really enjoy, that you're good at, that would make life worth living? What is it that you really want out of life, that would make living in the present an easy habit to maintain?

## Question No. 4: What's the Price?

One of the realities of life is that we all have endless desires but very limited time. Therefore, what we want out of life isn't the only issue; the price of what we want has to be figured into the equation. This should not be viewed as a negative, because if everything in life were easy—if success came without a price tag—it would be hard to appreciate anything. For example, what gives life itself such a high value is death. Therefore, we find it worthwhile to pay almost any price necessary to stay alive. There are many things we would like to do, but because we know they would endanger or shorten our lives, we refrain from doing them.

When considering what you want out of life, you have to give the price serious consideration. The price can present itself in many forms, such as time, energy, pain, and/or sacrifice. Sacrifice is an inescapable price because of the Natural Law of Balance; i.e., there always is an offsetting negative to every positive situation. Your foremost desire in life may conflict sharply with many other things you want, and sacrificing those other things could be a significant part of the cost. For example, you may have to sacrifice recreation, relaxation, and/or time with your family.

Also, human nature being what it is, the price of success usually includes having to endure the jealousy and resentment of others. It can get pretty ugly at times, often draining you of limited supplies of time and energy. Some people have difficulty handling this kind of discomfort, so it's another reality that should be addressed in advance.

Which leads to the final question:

## Question No. 5: Am I Willing to Pay the Price?

This is the easiest of the questions to fool yourself on, because it's so easy to say *yes*. But a serious *yes* means that you're prepared to be totally dedicated to the pursuit you've chosen. You should be so committed to your purpose that you develop what Napoleon Hill referred to as "a white heat of desire."

Unfortunately, we can never know for certain how big the price is, or whether we're willing to pay it, until we're actually tested. In other words, the best we can do is believe that we're willing to pay the price, but it's up to events to prove us right or wrong. This, however, should not prevent you from making the best possible evaluation of your willingness ahead of time. Certainly, if you have doubts about the price in advance, the chances are pretty good that you'll bail out at the first sign of trouble.

So seeking a meaningful purpose to your life can be a tricky proposition. You may want something badly, but not badly enough to pay the necessary price. As I said earlier, this is why it's so important to know *why* you want something. It's the why that gives you the desire that in turn makes you willing to pay the price.

## Serious Business

When I was much younger, I felt that questions concerning goals and purpose in life were elementary at best. I held firmly to this kind of above-it-all attitude until well past the time I graduated from the Age-of-Infinite-Wisdom phase of my life. However, the more real-life experience I've accumulated, the more I've come to realize just how important are goals and purpose. As a result, I take very seriously the five Present Living Questions I've discussed in this chapter, and urge you to do the same. Making money is not that difficult once you've laid the proper foundation, but I'm convinced it's at the foundation that most people fall short.

Because I know all too well just how easy it is to become cavalier when it comes to studying the five Present Living Questions, I'd like to offer some suggestions on how to go about answering them.

First, force yourself to write down both the questions and answers, because that forces you to be clear. One of the most important rules a writer learns early in his career is that unclear writing is a sign of unclear thinking.

Second, to the extent possible you should do your thinking in a quiet, secluded area. Over the years, I've spent hundreds of hours looking out over the ocean and pondering the Present Living Questions.

Third, take all the time you need to think through both the questions and your answers. It's imperative that you not rush your answers, because it takes time to make certain that you aren't kidding yourself about them.

Fourth, avoid discussing these questions with friends or relatives. It's not that they aren't well-meaning; on the contrary, they usually are. It's just that the more you discuss them with other people, the less likely it is that the answers will be yours.

And, finally, never forget that the one absolutely certain thing about life is that circumstances continually change, so periodically step back and review your progress, and if you don't seem to be getting where you want to be in life, reevaluate your answers. This is perhaps the most important point of all, because human beings are in a continual state of change. This causes our priorities to change, too, often without our being consciously aware of it.

For example, a person may at one point in his life be unwilling to pay the price of traveling and being away from his family several days a week. But when his children reach their teenage years, that may no longer be a major consideration. (In fact, he may *jump* at the chance to get away from his teenage children.) In my case, I remember when making money was my main objective. However, making money as an end in itself long ago dropped completely off my list of priorities. Why? Because I learned that money, like happiness, is but a side effect of pursuing a meaning in life. To the extent one has a purposeful life, making money becomes a rather easy proposition.

This is such an important principle that it's impossible to overemphasize it. If I can save just one reader the wasted time, energy, and unhappiness that result from being imprisoned by the will to money, the repetition is worth it. Do not allow yourself to get caught in this insidious trap. It's a lot harder to get out than it is to get in.

## The Bonus

Finally, I'd like to point out that one of the nice bonuses to having a meaningful purpose in life, and in turn being able to live in the present, is something I refer to as the Success Cycle. The Success Cycle is the antithesis of the so-called vicious, or failure, cycle. As with the habits that bring it about, the essence of the Success Cycle is quite simple:

The more certain you are about your purpose in life, the more focused you'll be on living in the present and the more enthusiastic you'll be in your day-to-day work; the more you display the Present Living Habit and enthusiasm in your daily work, the more likely you will attract the attention of positive, enthusiastic people; the more positive, enthusiastic people you attract, the more successful you'll be; and the more successful you are, the more present-living oriented and enthusiastic you'll be. Thus you set in motion a self-perpetuating cycle of enthusiasm and success. This cycle in turns adds fuel to the dynamic mental process that draws to you the things, people, and circumstances needed to translate the mental image of what you want out of life into physical reality.

# Chapter 5

# The Morality Habit

One of the earmarks of a civilization is a generally accepted moral code, or standard of behavior, upon which most of that civilization's laws are based. Ideally, I agree with the philosophy that every individual should have the right to take whatever action he chooses, so long as he doesn't forcibly interfere with the rights of others. In the real world, however, idealism is fantasy.

The reason there is a perceived need for morally based laws is that there is widespread disagreement as to when the actions of one individual impinge on the rights of others. For example, if there were no generally accepted code of conduct (i.e., if we lived in a totally free society), a person would have the right to walk down the street with no clothes on. Such an individual could argue that he is neither committing aggression against anyone nor trying to convert others to his way of thinking, so he should be allowed to do as he pleases. However, most people would disagree with this viewpoint and insist that such a person's actions do infringe on their rights. They might justifiably argue that they are, in essence, being forced to view something that they deem to be obscene or, at the very least, unpleasant.

I bring up this philosophical point because it presents a fundamental problem with regard to consistency in your day-to-day conduct. There are probably a great many morally based laws on the books with which you disagree. By the same token, there are actions that are technically legal which you may believe should be outlawed on moral grounds. A tough question to tackle, then, is whether or not you should obey laws that you feel are immoral.

Back to the subject of reality: We must continue to remind ourselves that we are not operating in an ideal laboratory stocked with rational people brimming over with rational thoughts. If you ignore this reality, you do so at your own peril. Man-made laws are a reality, regardless of whether or not they are rational or moral, and regardless of whether or not you or I like them. Therefore, within reason, and to the extent possible, you should attempt to obey man-made laws if only because it is pragmatic to do so. It's extremely difficult to achieve any great degree of success from inside a prison cell.

With these prefacing remarks as a caveat, I now emphasize the other side of the moral coin: Though you may choose to obey certain laws for pragmatic reasons, that should have little or no effect on your *personal* moral beliefs. On the contrary, an important key to success is to define clearly your own set of moral standards as a guide to your daily behavior, while not losing sight of the realities of man-made laws. Put another way, you should be honest because you *want* to, not because you *have* to.

## The Necessity for Clear Values

Defining your moral standards serves as an ethical compass that prevents you from straying off course when the winds of temptation begin howling around your ship of life. Millions of people continually crash on the rocks of bad consequences, often suffering irreparable damage, because they allowed themselves to get caught in rough waters without first making certain that they had their ethical compasses aboard.

It's imperative to understand that for any strategy or plan of action to be sound, it must begin with a solid moral foundation. Without such a foundation, anything a person tries to build is destined to crumble. The bad effect of a bad cause may not show up immediately, but you can be certain that ultimately it will make its appearance. When I speak of establishing a strong moral foundation, I mean developing a clear set of values that predetermines your day-to-day behavior. You need to know what you believe in ahead of time in order to understand why you should do things a certain way. What do you believe is moral? What do you believe is immoral? What do you believe is ethical? What do you believe is unethical? What do you believe is good? What do you believe is evil?

If you don't formulate your moral beliefs ahead of time, your actions may inadvertently be based on spur-of-the-moment whims, on emotion, or on immediate gratification. In other words, you're likely to revise your ethical standards to fit each new situation as it arises, a practice commonly referred to as "situational ethics." An individual who engages in situational ethics is someone who does not possess a fixed standard of right and wrong. Right is simply whatever he perceives to be in his immediate best interest at any given time, which is a foolproof formula for failure. It's imperative that you decide on a clear, concise set of moral values while your intellect is in control. Then in highly emotional situations you're more likely to act in accordance with the moral standards that you have decided—in advance—to live by.

## The Overriding Issue

(In this chapter, I purposely do not address morality as it relates to areas such as drugs, pornography, and abortion. These are hot topics for debate, and in a large percentage of cases are tied to the spiritual beliefs of the debaters. However, these topics are beyond the scope of this book.)

In my view, the key moral issue that needs to be addressed for purposes of this book is honesty. Plain and simple, honesty is the absolute refusal to lie, steal, cheat, or deceive in any way. Admittedly, that's a pretty rigid definition. Does it mean that we're all dishonest? Yes, because, as human beings, we're all imperfect. Actually, it would be more proper to say that each of us defines *lie*, *steal*, *cheat*, and *deceive* in our own way.

What follows constitutes *my* subjective views regarding honesty, and I offer these views only as food for thought. In the final analysis, however, you must formulate your own guidelines regarding honesty in order to acquire the Morality Habit in a meaningful way. What's most important is that you formulate your guidelines in advance, before being confronted with a situation that appeals to your immediate-gratification instincts.

The terms *lie*, *steal*, *cheat*, and *deceive* tend to overlap, so in discussing honesty I won't attempt to distinguish among them. For brevity's sake, most of my comments are focused on the subject of lying, but keep in mind that when one lies, one is often equally guilty of stealing, cheating, and deceiving, as well.

I have made no attempt to address such areas as "The Big Lie," compulsive lying, premeditated lying, or malevolent lying, because I assume that the reader's intentions are good and that he is basically honest. The person with bad intentions— who *plans* to be dishonest—has a completely different set of problems that also are beyond the scope of this book. Good intentions are a given; however, good intentions are not enough. To win in the real world, sound moral practices must be *implemented* through force of habit.

## The Little White Lie

All of us tell what are commonly known as *little white lies*, or what I like to refer to as "convenience lies." A person would have to possess a very severe case of Self-Righteousness Syndrome to believe that he is never guilty of telling little white lies. For example, when you tell your secretary to tell Mr. Smith that you're not in, but you're actually at your desk, the reality is that you're lying. Perhaps someone may want to challenge me on this point and insist that I'm being too technical, that something so insignificant shouldn't be considered a lie. Let's examine it more closely and see if he's right:

Were you in your office when Mr. Smith called?

"Yes."

Were you sitting at your desk?

"Yes."

Did you tell your secretary to tell Mr. Smith you weren't in?

"Yes."

Well, was your statement true or false?

To this last question, many people might be inclined to answer, "Okay, okay. It was false, but I wasn't lying."

Talk about self-delusion, the reality is that a knowingly false statement *is* a lie, no matter how insignificant it may be in your eyes.

To put an exclamation point on the subtlety of the little white lie, let's look at a commonly practiced nonbusiness example that virtually everyone can relate to:

When a parent tells a ticket seller at a movie theater that his thirteen-year-old son is only twelve because he wants to pay less for the child's ticket, he's lying. Worse, the child makes a mental note of the fact that his parent lied. Millions of parents delude themselves about seemingly trivial issues like this, not thinking of such actions as lying, then wonder why their children turn around and practice deception on *them*. Such parents attempt to shield their consciousness from the reality that actions have consequences, and that children pay far more attention to what parents *do* than to what they *say*.

**Real-World Rule No. 274: The problem with little white lies is that they tend to lead to bigger and bigger lies, which in turn lead to more and more negative results.** Doesn't the unfaithful spouse often start by cheating on his mate only reluctantly and sparingly? Doesn't the bank robber usually begin by shoplifting as a youth? Dishonest actions initially may seem innocent, reluctant, and/or inconsequential, but almost without exception they mushroom. Morality is the concept of right and wrong. You either believe that lying, stealing, cheating, and deceiving are right, or you believe they are wrong. If they're wrong, then technically they are *never* morally justified.

## The Exaggeration Lie

Another common form of lying that most people don't normally think of as lying is *exaggeration*. Nothing makes me lose confidence in a person more quickly than to discover that he's inflated his facts or feats.

One must be ever vigilant when it comes to exaggeration lies, because, like little white lies, they often wear an ever so subtle mask. For example, a little thing like leaving so-called urgent messages for people is usually an exaggeration lie. To my way of thinking, the word *urgent* implies something close to a life-and-death matter. If the message really isn't urgent, then the person who leaves such a message sustains a substantial loss of credibility. The same is true when you tell someone that if he'll meet with you, you'll take only five minutes of his time, then you end up taking thirty minutes. As a result, you gain a well-deserved reputation as the boy who cries wolf, and you don't get in the door again.

### THE $100,000-A-YEAR SALESMAN

Say that a real estate salesman tells you he made "about $100,000" last year. (Did you ever notice that *all* real estate salespeople made "about $100,000" last year—never $50,000 or $75,000, but always "about $100,000"?) On closer scrutiny, however, you find that the figure wasn't quite $100,000. It really was $88,000, but the salesman conveniently rounded it off on the high side—and that was in *gross commissions*. However, since most sales commissions are split with another brokerage firm, that left him only about $44,000. The broker who employs the salesman then got half of the $44,000 as his cut, which left the salesman with only $22,000.

But there's still a little something called "overhead" to be figured in. (You know what overhead is—that mysterious cost phenomenon unique to *your* business. No one else has overhead, right?) So by the time the $100,000-a-year salesman deducts incidentals such as gas, auto maintenance, supplies, treating prospects to lunch and dinner, and various other miscellaneous expenses, what he really *netted* was a grand total of $8,422.87—quite a comedown from $100,000!

To top it off, this year things aren't going nearly as well for this salesman, so if you follow him home some evening, don't be surprised to find that he's moved from his sparsely furnished studio apartment into a medium-sized tent. The truth is that it's a semantic error to refer to his "made about $100,000 last year" statement as an exaggeration, because it evades the real issue. In point of fact, it is an *exaggeration lie*.

## A FREE SHINE

A final example of exaggeration lying that stands out in my mind occurred when I was in New Orleans to speak at a hard-money financial conference. The evening I was scheduled to speak, I was still in my bathrobe in my hotel suite, preparing to shave, when I heard a knock at the door. I opened it and, to my surprise, found the then governor of California, Jerry Brown, staring me in the face. He had been brought to my room by a mutual acquaintance, Michael, who was a very political animal. Michael had always been obsessed with gaining the friendship of politicians (remember, mental illness can take many forms), and he himself had made an unsuccessful bid for a congressional seat in his district.

As he walked through the door, Michael enthusiastically introduced Governor Brown to me, then bellowed, "Jerry, Robert is the guy I told you about who has a million of his newsletter readers' names on computer." It was a great introduction, except for one thing: Michael and I had discussed my newsletter list on several occasions, and he knew full well that the figure was more in the area of thirty thousand names. It didn't take any great amount of genius to figure out that he was trying to impress Governor Brown with his connections to people who owned valuable mailing lists that could lead to something spelled *c-o-n-t-r-i-b-u-t-i-o-n-s*. As Governor Brown dropped to the floor and began buffing my slippers with his iridescent purple and orange tie, my instinctive urge was to correct Michael's gross overstatement. However, within a few minutes he had reemphasized the figure *one million* at least twice, so it was a very awkward situation for me. Besides, I liked the way my slippers were coming out. Nonetheless, Michael's blatant exaggeration made it clear to me that nothing he ever said in the future could be taken at face value.

When it comes to fighting off the temptation to exaggerate, it's wise to practice the wisdom of **Real-World Rule No. 74: Always let people be surprised that you gave them more than you promised, faster than you promised, and that it was easier than you promised.** When you operate in this fashion, you'll stand out from the rest of the crowd like a thinking man at a Ted Kennedy rally.

## The Omission Lie

Omitting relevant information—the *omission lie*—is one of the most frequently employed forms of lying, and one of the most difficult to reconcile. It's tricky business because certainly you're not obligated to tell every person with whom you have dealings everything about your life. The guideline I use to determine whether or not something should be omitted (i.e., whether or not I have a moral obligation to volunteer certain information) is to ask myself: Will the other party draw wrong conclusions and thereby make decisions injurious to himself as a result of his not knowing about something I've withheld? If so, then the omission would be a lie.

Admittedly, this is a less than precise guideline, which is why lying through omission is so difficult to monitor. Much of it is in the eyes of the beholder, but the important thing is to get into the habit of trying. However, most cases of lying through omission are not borderline; they are blatant.

In the early 1970s, a business associate and I bought controlling interest in an American Stock Exchange company after prolonged negotiations with the major shareholders. On the surface, the company appeared to be very strong, with an 11-to-1 current ratio and about $4 million cash in the bank. In addition, sales of the company's main product line were represented on the books (and had been verbally confirmed) to be very strong.

What we were not told, however—and did not discover until long after we had purchased our shares—was that the high sales volume was misleading, because abnormally high product returns were anticipated in the coming year. (The company's products were sold to stores strictly on a consignment basis.) As a result, the company actually was in the early stages of a downturn. Soon after we became involved, it began to experience record returns far in excess of the reserves it had maintained on its books, and the results were a devastating blow to our plans.

As an aid to keeping my own moral behavior in the area of omissions in line, I periodically remind myself of this classic example of intentional lying through omission. Actions do have consequences, and, over the long haul, omission liars, like all other liars, suffer the consequences they deserve. The safest, simplest, day-to-day rule to follow in this area is: When in doubt, *don't* leave it out.

## The Sort-of-True Lie

The *sort-of-true lie* is used most effectively by those who have honed their lying skills to a point where they are super smooth at their craft. If an individual on this level gets caught, he can always argue that what he said was "sort of true," or that he "must have misunderstood what you were asking."

A young entrepreneur, Larry, once visited me to discuss a business proposal. By virtue of his marathon remarks throughout our meeting, it became obvious that he was still well entrenched in the Age-of-Infinite-Wisdom period of his life. He clearly was suffering from a severe case of delusions of grandeur, telling me, among other things, about his ambition to ultimately get into politics (my eyes slowly rolling toward the ceiling on cue) and "make an impact on the world." As he spoke, I thought to myself that perhaps he should begin with a somewhat less ambitious goal than impacting the whole world. Considering his credentials, stirring up the people of Buffalo seemed perhaps a more realistic objective.

During the course of our meeting, Larry repeated a point I had heard him make to a large group of people at an earlier date—that he had recently written a self-help book in a record thirty days. This was a task, he pointed out, that had taken an enormous amount of commitment, determination, and perseverance. I certainly agreed. When I had first heard him tell the story of how he had accomplished this incredible feat, I, like the rest of his audience, had been awed. However, because I had already authored a number of books myself, I, *unlike* the others in attendance, was also very skeptical.

Sure enough, not long after our one-on-one meeting, a friend happened to mention the details of how Larry's book actually had been written, exactly as he had heard it from the professional writer *who had ghostwritten the book*, including the amount of money the ghostwriter had been paid to do the job! What the writer had been instructed to do was distill Larry's seminar notes and put them together in book form. When I heard this, it occurred to me that if someone ever confronted this young entrepreneur with the facts, he could always argue that he had "sort of" written the book . . . in a way, that is . . . or perhaps all the people who had heard him say he had written it had just "misunderstood" what he really had meant by "I wrote my book in thirty days" . . . mumble, mumble, mumble . . . ad

infinitum. The sort-of-true lie is part little white lie, part exaggeration lie, and part omission lie.

A person who insists on telling sort-of-true lies should at least
pick his spots carefully. If he can't resist the urge to shade the
truth, at least he should learn to be selective with regard to
whom he tells his fairy tales. The problem with massaging the
truth with someone like me is that I'm one of those annoying
individuals who gets around too much. I know far too many
people, and have a Colombo-like habit of stumbling onto the
facts. If you're determined to lie, it's wise to restrict your lying
to people who stay in bed all day.

All lies have one thing in common, and that's the price you
pay when you're caught. And make no mistake about it, sooner
or later you *will* be caught, which results in the most difficult of
all losses to recoup—loss of credibility. The best protection
against making an exception to your moral code just to get by in
an uncomfortable situation is to keep reminding yourself that in
the real world, actions do indeed have consequences.

## Concentricity

*Integrity* is an impressive-sounding word, one that most people
use quite freely. Unfortunately, very few people really understand what the word means, and even fewer practice it. Integrity is adherence to your code of moral values. It's one thing to
talk about moral values, but quite another to consistently adhere to them. Integrity gets at the very heart of the Morality
Habit issue.

During a question-and-answer period at one of my seminars,
a gentleman said he believed that all government spending,
with the exception of expenditures for the protection of lives
and property, was theft, and therefore immoral. He confessed
that he felt guilty because he was a builder of government
housing (meaning his income was derived from money extracted
primarily from unwilling individuals, euphemistically referred
to as "taxpayers"). It was a lucrative business for him, and he

was in a quandary as to what to do. He asked me if I thought it was wrong for him to continue to profit from this kind of business.

In a way, I resented his question, because he knew full well what the answer was, and I felt he was hoping I would grant him dispensation and make everything all right. First of all, I don't have the power to grant dispensations, nor does any other human being. Integrity is a highly personal matter; you embrace it for your own sake. A hundred priests, ministers, and rabbis can forgive you, but all that matters is whether or not you can forgive yourself. There's only one way to protect your integrity: You must be ever vigilant when it comes to not compromising it. There is no other method I know of that works.

I'm talking about how well you practice what you claim to believe in. What you believe in and what you say is one thing; what you *do* is quite another. I like to think of this consistency of belief, words, and actions as *concentricity*. Try to imagine two perfect circles, one representing what you believe in and what you say, the other representing what you actually do. When these two circles are nearly concentric—that is, when they're almost perfectly aligned—it means that you're adhering to your code of moral values. But when the two circles begin to pull apart, it indicates that your integrity is slipping. And when what you do begins to pull too far away from what you believe in and what you say, you may find yourself looking in the mirror one morning and realizing that you're beginning to dislike and disrespect yourself. At first, you may not be able to figure out why, but if your intent is to be honest, the reason will soon emerge.

Again, I acknowledge that we're all human, which means we're imperfect, so it's simply not possible for these two circles ever to be 100 percent concentric. But that's precisely why you have to work hard at concentricity every day of your life. It's the only way you can hope to adhere to your values on a consistent basis. The temptations to allow those two circles to pull apart are everywhere, so it often takes tremendous self-discipline to hold them together. This is particularly true when it comes to

# CONCENTRICITY

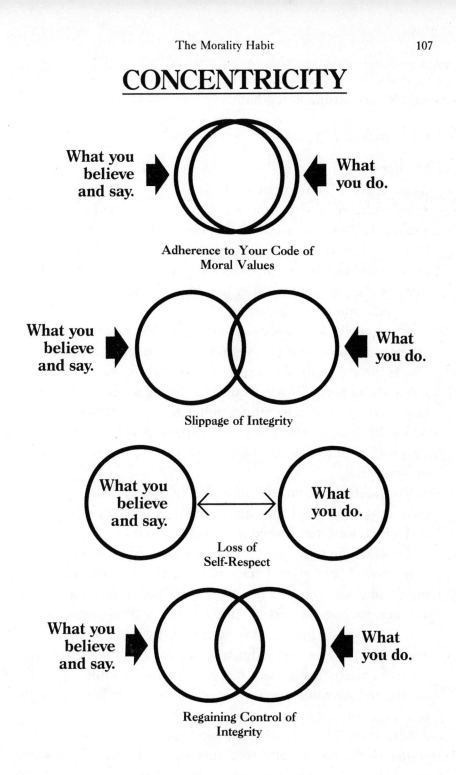

What you believe and say.  →  ←  What you do.

Adherence to Your Code of
Moral Values

What you believe and say.  →  ←  What you do.

Slippage of Integrity

What you believe and say.  ←→  What you do.

Loss of
Self-Respect

What you believe and say.  →  ←  What you do.

Regaining Control of
Integrity

omission lies and sort-of-true lies. Concentricity must become a way of life, an ingrained habit.

## Case-by-Case Basis

During a seminar tour I did a few years ago, I found myself faced with a difficult problem. In one of the cities in which I was going to be speaking, time was running short and we had neglected to arrange for our audio needs. Just before arriving in that city, I made a couple of quick phone calls and was referred to an individual at a local audio company. I immediately called him, but as the conversation unfolded, some of the things he said made me very uncomfortable.

At one point he emphasized that whenever I called I should ask only for him, and also should be sure not to talk to anyone else at the company about this particular audio job. "Hold on," I thought to myself, "what's this guy trying to tell me?" I asked him, "Now, let me be sure I understand something. Are you doing this job on behalf of your company or are you doing it on your own?" Sure enough, he told me that he was doing the job on his own.

"Well, then," I pressed forward, "if you're doing it on your own, how do you decide which jobs should go to your company and which jobs you should keep for yourself?"

To which he replied, "Oh, I take it on a case-by-case basis."

By now I was sorry I had initiated the inquiry, because I didn't like the results and there wasn't enough time to find another good audio person. Immediately I tried to rationalize, and I almost had myself convinced that it wasn't my problem. I told myself, "Hey, all I did was call someone who had been recommended to me, ask him if he could handle my audio needs, and anything else is none of my business. It's not my job to be the moral policeman of the world."

Man does, indeed, inhabit a world of delusions. What I was trying to do was "make true that which I loved," i.e., that which was convenient to my short-term needs. As the hours rolled by, I felt those two circles almost flying in opposite directions. I took a good look in the mirror, and, sure enough, there he was—Richard Nixon staring back at me.

Well, maybe not quite that bad, but I sure didn't like what I saw. I thought about the matter long and hard the rest of the day, and finally had to admit that I was guilty of trying to delude myself. Standing in front of an audience and preaching the importance of having a solid moral foundation, while at the same time knowing that the person who was recording me was at that very moment engaging in a blatantly dishonest act, was at a minimum hypocritical and at worst flat-out dishonest on my part. Any way I sliced it, the reality was that I would knowingly be helping someone to lie, steal, cheat, and deceive his employer.

At the eleventh hour, I managed to save my self-respect by mustering the courage to call and cancel the technician's services. In relating this story, I said there "wasn't enough time to find another good audio person." What I really had meant, but didn't want to admit to myself, was that it would be *difficult* to find another good audio person on such short notice. But there's a big difference between *difficult* and *impossible*. It's the ultimate rationalization, and many people manage to rationalize their way through life by continually playing this subtle, self-delusive trick on themselves.

The point is that anyone can be honest when it doesn't cause him inconvenience or discomfort, particularly when money is involved. When your honesty is really on the line, though, is when adhering to your moral beliefs causes you great hardship or inconvenience. That's why you have to think through your moral beliefs ahead of time and develop the habit of sticking to those beliefs. Then, when the moment of truth arrives, you won't even have to stop to think about the proper course of action.

To strengthen your concentricity, I suggest you need **Real-World Rule No. 211: The surest way to get good results in this life, and to go to Heaven in the next life, is to live every moment as though the whole world were watching.** In other words, if you live the same kind of life in private that you live when you're in the company of others, your actions will become consistent through force of habit.

## Consider the Source

This brings up the sticky problem of people sometimes thinking you're dishonest even though *you* don't believe you've done anything wrong. What should you do if someone falsely accuses you of an immoral action?

For starters, your frame of reference should be that it's far more important to *be* honest than to have everyone *think* you're honest. In an imperfect world, the reality is that you can neither please everyone nor get everyone to like you. Therefore, the first thing you should do is consider the source. Look at it this way: Have you ever dealt with a dishonest person? Of course you have. Second question: Have you ever had anyone admit to you that he's dishonest? Have you ever had anyone say to you, "Honesty compels me to admit that I'm dishonest." It's never happened, right?

So what's at the root of this seeming contradiction? Well, if you consider someone else to be dishonest, that same person is almost certain to think that you're dishonest, because your moral standards are different from his. Worse, often your accuser doesn't even know you, which can add even more irritation to the accusation.

Therefore, you should not allow it to get you down if you're attacked by someone whose moral standards are different from yours. Instead, I suggest you take the advice of one of the wisest men I've ever known, who once explained to me a very sound approach to handling unjust accusations. He said that if someone falsely accuses you, just look in the mirror and say to yourself, "If my hands are clean, and my cause is just, and my demands are reasonable, I have nothing to worry about." Then simply go about your business.

At the extreme, your honest actions may sometimes make others mad, particularly in situations in which people want you to cooperate with them in an act that you consider to be immoral. You should never kid yourself about your honest actions being appreciated by everyone. In our world of delusions, the reality is that integrity doesn't always make a person popular, but it does give him the greatest of all assets, one that money can't purchase: Unwavering integrity makes a person *free*, and nothing could be a more positive result than that.

When it comes to the Morality Habit, the wise person refuses to compromise his integrity for anybody or anything. To the extent the Morality Habit becomes ingrained, such a person greatly enhances his chances of achieving high-level success.

# Chapter 6

# The Human Relations Habit

Like it or not—and many people don't—to one extent or another you have to deal with others to achieve any reasonable degree of success. This is true regardless of your station in life and no matter what your objectives may be. Further, the more successful you are in getting others to cooperate with you, and the more people you can solicit as allies, the greater your chances of achieving positive results. It can sometimes get very lonely and brutal in the Malevolent Jungle when those wild herds of humanoids start stampeding your homestead.

The issue of good human relations is pretty simple: To the extent you relate poorly to others, you tend to have a problem-filled life, and success comes hard, if at all; to the extent you relate well to others, you tend to have a pleasant life, and success comes relatively easy.

An individual can be brilliant at many things, yet be totally ignorant when it comes to getting along with, and gaining the cooperation of, others. Everyone knows someone who is knowledgeable about a wide variety of subjects, but seemingly has zero knowledge of human relations. In most cases, it's because the otherwise knowledgeable individual has not taken the trouble to study human relations, or even to give the subject much thought. That's unfortunate, because, like all other habits, superior human relations is an art that anyone can learn. Some people may be born with more natural talent in this area than others, but that's true of virtually everything in life. More important is the fact that anyone can become better through practice.

At least two major pluses accrue to your benefit when you become adept at relating well to others:

First, by understanding the techniques involved in successful human relations, you attract others who appreciate these same techniques. If you make it a habit to practice those things that make you an attractive human being, you will appeal to other attractive human beings, and attractive human beings add value to your life.

Second, when you're strong in the area of human relations, you gain the cooperation of others, and this cooperation is the shortest distance between you and your goals. It's the flip side of a friction-filled life. When too many people are pulling against you, rooting against you, and begrudging your success, it's like being stalked by an endless wave of Pacmen. Actions have consequences: If you treat people in negative ways, they will act negatively toward you; if you treat people in positive ways, they will act positively toward you. If that sounds simple, it's because it is. In fact, it's one of the simplest known methods for getting results, which is why it's remarkable that so few people make the effort to develop good human relations.

Many self-development authors make the mistake of urging readers to display qualities such as self-esteem in their relations with others. However, as with a positive mental attitude, self-esteem cannot be willed. When someone says, "You should display self-esteem," he really is saying, "You should *fake* self-esteem." In point of fact, a quality such as self-esteem is a *result* of practicing good human relations. Likewise, feelings toward you that emanate from others—such as love and respect—cannot be willed. They, too, are a *result* of successful human relations.

When you master the Human Relations Habit, it leads to a

triple win: You make others feel better; you feel better; and, directly or indirectly, your goodwill toward others will come back to you with interest somewhere down the liferoad.

## Keys to the Cooperation Vault

Many of the qualities and actions that lead to superior human relations are inextricably tied to effective communication. The longer I live, the more I see life as an ongoing series of miscommunications between human beings. For example, no matter how much concern you may feel for another person, you still have to communicate that concern to him. In order to achieve successful human relations, you must be successful in communicating qualities such as those discussed in this chapter. To merely philosophize about them is insufficient; they must be implemented, through both words and actions.

Following are some of the more important traits that must become habits if one is to gain the cooperation and goodwill of others. The list is by no means complete, but it is more than extensive enough for our purposes. To one extent or another, you likely are already familiar with each of the traits on the list; after all, learning is often just a matter of finding out what you already know. Thus, my primary objective in discussing these traits is to motivate you to move your performance in the area of human relations up several notches.

### Brevity

Nothing embarrasses me more than when I leave a meeting feeling that I've overdramatized my points by being childishly redundant. People tend to be skeptical about the lady who "doth protest too much." We would all do well to remember the words of David Ogilvy: "When a company boasts about its integrity, or a woman about her virtue, avoid the former and cultivate the latter." Busy people are impatient, so when you have something to say, be succinct, keep it simple, say exactly what you mean—then stop.

In both your personal and business dealings, it's wise to heed **Real-World Rule No. 148: The power of the understatement is enormous.** That which is well said is quickly said. If it's something positive, it will be that much better received if presented in a brief manner. If it's a negative, it will be less painful if it isn't dragged out. Just as unclear writing is a sign of unclear thinking, verbal rambling is a sign of not having your thoughts organized.

Brevity is particularly vital when it comes to making business proposals. People get uneasy if they can't understand what you're talking about, so learn to stick to the facts. When you make a presentation, there are only three relevant issues that need to be addressed:

1. What, specifically, do you want from me?

2. If I give you what you want, what specifically do you expect to accomplish with it?

3. If you accomplish everything you hope to, specifically what's in it for me and what's in it for you?

Experience has taught me that when you're dealing with successful people, almost everything else you have to say is extraneous. This is especially true when you're trying to raise money. Avoid being superfluous, and don't waste time on side comments designed to patronize or butter up the other party. The chances are good that he didn't acquire money to invest in the first place without being pretty sharp, so don't try to be cute with him. Always remember the advice contained in **Real-World Rule No. 267: Never try to promote a promoter!**

## Compassion

Though you cannot will someone to have compassion for you, *you* can learn to have compassion for *others*. Compassion really involves nothing more than putting yourself in the other person's shoes and trying to feel what he's experiencing. Thoreau was right about most people living lives of quiet desperation. The average person is in pain, and if you don't take that factor into consideration before speaking or acting, you can neither help others nor can you gain their cooperation. To paraphrase Jim Rohn, a speaker with a knack for graphically verbalizing a point, you have to "meet people in the hurt."

As with everything in life, you'll reap just about what you sow when it comes to compassion, and the least you'll gain from being compassionate is a heightened sense of self-esteem. More likely, however, you'll reap many additional rewards, both directly and indirectly, as time passes. Compassion is a common language that links together the goodwill members of the human race, helping to offset widespread negative traits such as hatred and contempt.

If it's true that every twenty-four hours the world turns over and somebody new is on top, it's also true that somebody new is on the bottom. Fortune tires of carrying anyone on its shoulders too long, and, as thousands of megamillionaires during the past decade have found, no one is immune to financial disaster. When such disaster descends upon a Leona Helmsley type, the afflicted individual quickly discovers there is much truth to the axiom "Everything that goes around comes around."

In a world that operates religiously within a framework of actions and consequences, the person who demonstrates the most compassion *toward* others is the person who is destined to reap the most compassion *from* others. Making it a habit to be compassionate costs nothing but is worth everything.

## Decisiveness

I've had to work hard to nurture this habit over the years, particularly when people have tried to pressure me into committing to something that I really didn't want to do. I often used to say things like, "Let me think about it," or "Give me a call in a couple of weeks," which I now realize was very weak on my part. The result was that people would end up getting angry at me, while the guy who refused to yield to pressure and gave a flat *no* right off the bat would be long forgotten.

One day I was lamenting to a friend how I had gotten myself into a jam with someone, even though I had not told the person that I would go along with his request. My friend really opened my eyes when he said, "The reason you get into tight situations like this is that you egg people on. Instead of giving them a rigid *no* the first time they ask, you try to mumble your way out of situations and leave them up in the air. I think you're just afraid to give people a firm and final *no*."

I always take criticism well, so after throwing a lamp at my friend, I objectively pondered his views and concluded that he was absolutely right. I now recognize that it's a matter of sacrificing the short-term comfort of avoiding embarrassment, or possible negative vibrations, in exchange for long-term peace of mind—i.e., knowing that the matter has been permanently resolved. To boot, the other person ends up liking you more, not less, for having been firm with him from the outset. You didn't give him false hope (always a breeding ground for ill feelings), and didn't waste his time. In addition, you're able to completely forget about the matter and go about your business with a clear mind.

## Discretion

A discreet person exercises sound judgment when it comes to guarding private matters, using discretion in both words and actions. What makes discretion so important is a little reality of life called *human nature*. To the extent we ignore this reality, we reap negative results.

It's human nature for people to want that which is least accessible to them, and to be indifferent about that which is most available. To the degree you overexpose yourself, you become an inflated commodity, which in turn causes a devaluation of you in the eyes of others. Neither you nor I have anything to say about it; it's human nature that controls the issue.

In his book *Power! How To Get It, How To Use It,* Michael Korda states bluntly, "No matter who you are, the basic truth is that your interests are nobody else's concern." The most poorly received words in the English language are *I, me,* and *my.* Some people display an almost childish naïveté in this regard, appearing to believe that everyone in the world is interested in the wart on their big toe or the fact that their dog had puppies last week. The well-adjusted individual separates himself from such self-centered fantasy early in life. In fact, one of life's great crises is in coming to grips with the reality that our affairs simply aren't that important to others.

Inundating people with your problems is an especially self-destructive lack-of-discretion habit to harbor. Human nature makes it a certainty that this practice will badly tarnish your image with those unlucky souls who are on the listening end. Also, fewer people will want to deal with you, because it's human nature for people to keep their distance from those enshrouded by problems. The more you talk about your problems, the worse your chances of attracting positive people, which makes it that much harder to *solve* your problems. Even if a person is your friend, it's a grave mistake to babble on endlessly about the details of your private life, because familiarity really does breed contempt.

Likewise, it's a lack of discretion to announce your plans to the world. There are too many envious and malevolent people out there who would just love to see you trip (preferably breaking three or four toes in the process). If your plans should yield the results you're hoping for, the world will hear about them soon enough. But—horror of horrors—if you should completely flop, why give card-carrying members of the World Order of Malevolent Mammals something else to cheer about? Avoid revealing the heart of your enterprise to more people than are absolutely necessary to bring about its success. He who postpones declaring his purpose, particularly if it involves a major undertaking, envelops his actions in a veil of mystery that commands respect. A plan fully declared is rarely well thought of, and is fair game for criticism. Instead of arousing universal expectations, let people wonder and watch.

This is especially true when you're confident that you have a deal wrapped up. It's the height of indiscretion to celebrate prematurely. Again, the surest way to invite trouble into your life and to get malevolent people thinking about possible ways to derail you is to spout off about results prematurely. Never confuse the term *almost done* with the word *done*. There's a big difference between the two. **Real-World Rule No. 224: You're not through until you've crossed all the t's and dotted all the i's and the check has cleared the bank.**

Unfortunately, there's no such thing as a smooth closing. Like a good pass receiver, you should acquire the habit of looking the pass into your hands before celebrating. I learned this lesson very early in my career when I managed to line up financing to build an apparel factory in Glenville, West Virginia. After working on the deal for months, the time finally arrived when I was able to get everyone involved to agree to a closing date. I was so excited, I was already counting the profits I was going to be earning in the coming years. Having only recently completed my journey through the Age of Infinite Wisdom, I boasted to everyone who would listen (an order taker at McDonald's, two derelicts on a park bench, and an attorney from Zaire) about my deal. At that early stage of my career, I wasn't familiar with the immortal words of that legendary Italian philosopher, Yogi Berra, who voiced his now famous truism: "It ain't over till it's over."

You think you know the finale, right? Well, in order to guess this one correctly, you'd have to be a closet sadist. The day before the closing I received a call from the secretary of the individual who was the key player in the financing of the project. Would you believe she was calling to tell me that her boss had suffered a fatal heart attack sitting at his desk—just twenty-four hours before the papers were to be signed and the money was to change hands? I was stunned. I'm telling you, some people will do *anything* to kill a deal!

Even when a deal does close (and, contrary to popular belief, it really does happen now and then), you still should avoid yakking to the world about how you managed to pull it off. Let people scratch their heads in awe. As Don Shimoda said in Richard Bach's *Illusions,* "Learn what the magician knows and it's not magic anymore."

## Genuineness

Genuineness lies in cultivating the habit of consciously trying to be your true self. The reality is that each of us is on stage to one degree or another through most of our lives. Just as it's impossible to be honest 100 percent of the time, neither is it possible for anyone to be himself always and completely. However, that doesn't mean that a person should not *strive* to be himself. In the best of cases, an individual still will fall short of his mark.

There's at least one serious problem with being "on" too much of the time, or to too much of an extreme: Not only do you continually run into yourself (in disguise) coming around every corner, but those who might like the real you won't get the opportunity to discover who that is. This is a serious problem because the biggest human relations dividends are reaped when you meet others who are most like you, in both your business and personal life.

Another nonbusiness example, one in which the moral is equally applicable to financial situations, illustrates what I mean:

In 1976, I was invited to a New Year's Eve party, and was wavering on whether or not to attend. I really dislike New Year's Eve parties, because I don't drink, don't dance, don't like to stay up late, and refuse to kiss strangers. I know, I know, you're thinking I'm not very exciting—and you're right.

Finally, Fate grabbed me by the throat and pulled me to my car, started the motor, and took me to the party. I stumbled around in my usual suave and sophisticated manner, exchanging pleasantries with total strangers and slowly losing the battle to keep my smile pasted on. People must have thought I had come from the Planet Square, because I seemed to be the only male in attendance who didn't have my shirt unbuttoned to the waist, wasn't dangling seven pounds of fake gold from my neck, and didn't have coiffed locks reaching down to my shoulders. Throughout the hip seventies, I stubbornly retained my Tommy Smothers hairstyle, to the great amusement of all who met me.

During the previous twelve months I had made a commitment to myself to grow up, be mature, and start dressing and acting like a middle-aged man—which you must admit is an astounding objective for a fully grown adult in Los Angeles. I was determined to be the real Robert Ringer, no matter how out of place I might feel in any given situation.

About an hour after midnight, I was fumbling my way toward the front door, looking forward to the solitude of my humble abode, when I happened to catch a glimpse of a face—the most beautiful face I had ever seen—across the room. My heart started jumping around in my chest like a pachinko ball, and I seriously considered taking a drink. She was sitting and talking to another young lady, and not only was she beautiful, she also was smiling nonstop.

"What should I do? How do I make contact?" I frantically asked the little character inside my wildly gyrating brain.

"Don't panic," he cautioned. "Just be yourself."

Be myself? That was too much to think about. This was a situation that required immediate action. As I continued to stare at her through the crowd, wild thoughts bombarded my mind. Perhaps I should extend my arm toward her and break into song: "Some enchanted evening . . . you will see a stranger . . ."

"But what if I trip just as I get to her? What if she looks at me like I'm crazy and gets up and leaves? Maybe I should jump up on the pillar behind her and break into something more upbeat, like 'Singin' in the Rain.' No, I might fall off, then I'd really look stupid."

Acutely aware that time was running out on an opportunity to meet my lifetime fantasy, I pulled myself together, patted my Smotherscut for unruly hairs, and marched resolutely toward her through the raucous, dancing crowd.

"I'll just be myself," I thought, "then take her insulting response in stride, go home like a man, and cry myself to sleep."

Within seconds, the moment arrived. Sitting next to her, I blurted out one of the great boy-girl lines in romantic history: "Hi!"

As I mentally flinched in anticipation of her sharp-tongued response, the lovely female looked at me, displayed an incredible affidavit smile, and in the most cheerful voice imaginable answered, "Hi!"

I was so taken aback that I didn't know how to react at first. After all, this was the land of gold chains and 450 SLs. Girls at parties weren't supposed to smile and be friendly—at least not until they checked your financial statement and movie credits. Then, if all the paperwork was in order and the female was feeling generous, she might be willing to exchange ten minutes' worth of sarcastic conversation with you.

"What's going on here?" I asked my little friend roaming about inside my skull. "Who in the world is this happy mermaid, anyway?"

"Just be yourself, stupid, and don't blow it," he admonished me.

She was the first female I had met in Freakland in years who displayed an obvious abundance of self-confidence and self-esteem. No defensiveness; no sarcasm; no demands that the other person submit a typewritten résumé. In this little corner of our planet, such an attitude is considered way out of the mainstream, even somewhat bizarre.

"What's your name? Where are you from?" Normal, simple

questions, with no thought given to how they might sound. Just honest, corny, straightforward stuff. It was absolutely great.

All I can remember is four hours of sitting and talking . . . walking around and talking . . . laughing and talking . . . and talking some more. When I finally departed at 5:00 A.M., there was no doubt in my mind that I had just met my future wife. Thirteen years have passed since that extraordinary New Year's Eve meeting, and my wife is still smiling, still the most natural, unspoiled, kind human being I have ever known. She comes the closest I've ever seen to a person who is never on stage. She's just as happy and down to earth in private as she is in public. She's sincere and caring whether she's dealing with a high-society matriarch or a clerk in a dilapidated shop in a Mexican pueblo.

As you can imagine, my wife and I have talked many times about our initial meeting, and we agree that had I tried to mimic the army of male mutants in attendance, fondling a gold chain and smirking as I approached her, it would have been a very short conversation. She would have had no idea what I really was like. Talk about a big payoff, this was one that dramatically changed my entire life for the better, and it was a direct result of practicing the habit of being genuine. Sometimes I have nightmares thinking about what might have happened had Woody Allen gotten to her first. It's too painful even to imagine.

The moral? Always remember that the hardest way to impress people is to *try* to impress people. You have to merit respect and let it come naturally. As a rule, the least amount of respect and praise comes your way when you seek it the most. Where a person gets into trouble is when he starts trying to be someone other than who he really is. People may or may not like who you really are, but they will *never* like you for trying to be someone *other* than who you are.

## Graciousness

Few things pay greater dividends in the area of human relations than the habit of exercising graciousness. Amazingly, even though it's simple to be kind and cordial to others, we live in a very ungracious world.

Graciousness is taking the time to return phone calls even if you don't think the caller possesses anything of value to you at the moment. I'm not referring to solicitors or total strangers, but to people you know or with whom you've had amiable dealings in the past. When you take the trouble to return calls in a timely fashion, it sets you apart from ungracious competitors and almost certainly will come back to you in the form of increased business.

Graciousness is praising someone if he's done a job well or accomplished an admirable feat. Everyone—and I do mean everyone—needs reassurance when it comes to his abilities and value. It's not a matter of flattery; rather, it's a matter of being thoughtful enough to speak sincere words of praise when such words are warranted.

Graciousness is taking the trouble to show gratitude to someone who has done you a favor or demonstrated kindness toward you. Again, showing appreciation for someone's nice gesture is an easy habit to develop, yet so rewarding both to you and to the recipient of your thanks. It's a sad commentary on our culture that a simple display of gratitude on your part can instantly catapult you to the head of another person's good-guy list.

This thought first struck me about twenty years ago when I sent personalized, initialed lucite paperweights to about fifty business acquaintances as Christmas gifts. I hadn't given any conscious thought to the recipients responding to my relatively expensive gifts when I sent them out, but when one person did call to thank me, human nature set in. Because one person—and one person only—did take the trouble to thank me, it got me to thinking about the other forty-nine who didn't. With a response like this, I began to wonder what the feedback might have been had I sent the same people live tarantulas. So, when next Christmas rolled around . . . (just kidding).

Now, you might be thinking, "Well, your main reason for sending gifts shouldn't have been to receive thanks from people." Aside and apart from the fact that, as I stated, I hadn't given any conscious thought to the recipients showing appreciation, what my motives may or may not have been completely misses the point. Regardless of my intent, the one individual who did take the trouble to thank me stood head and shoulders above the field. Had that individual been selling insurance, or office furniture, or any other product or service for which I was in the market, can you imagine what an easy sale I would have been for him? That's the real lesson to be learned from this little story. The person who makes a habit of a simple action like displaying gratitude can't help but reap benefits down the road, even if that isn't his main objective.

Graciousness also means not resorting to pettiness. In fact, your Pettiness Meter will give you an accurate reading of where you are in life at any particular time. The more a person is frustrated and failing, the more willing, even anxious, he is to waste time on petty matters. When your mind is filled with thoughts of defending yourself, how others have wronged you, and other similar petty impulses, you cannot simultaneously engage in positive or creative thinking. It's a matter of cultivating the habit of controlling your negative emotional impulses. Your daily energy supply is limited, so it's imperative that you practice converting negative, destructive energy into positive, creative energy.

Finally, graciousness means knowing how to win. The gracious person purposely avoids looking victorious over underlings, peers, and, above all, superiors. There's no worse blow to your relations with others than to display arrogance in victory. Many of the most successful people I know make it a habit to be gracious, polite, and considerate when they accomplish something outstanding. It's a wonderful insurance policy for staying on top.

## Refinement

Being refined is a matter of having good taste. There's nothing that breeds bad human relations quite as easily and quickly as being uncouth, rude, or vulgar.

To paraphrase an excellent example given by Zig Ziglar, in America a man is free to sport a Mohawk hairdo, dye it pink, wear a feathered earring in one ear, and spew out profanities. By the same token, employers are free not to hire him. By stretching his freedom to prove he can be as vulgar-looking as he desires, such a person also disqualifies himself from 90 percent or more of the employment opportunities that might otherwise be available to him. Unless you're a childish professional athlete, it's not a very pragmatic approach to life, and even athletes end up paying a steep price for being uncouth and outrageous when their playing days are over and they no longer can hide behind a uniform.

A few years ago, a young lady who had worked for me for only a few months asked if she could speak with me to air some grievances. I agreed to hear her out, whereupon she sat down and began to talk. After a few minutes of complaining that "Sue is doing this" and "Sally isn't doing that" (all about as relevant to her job as her ability to win at mud wrestling), she said, "I don't mind doing extra work, but I don't like being [expletive] over by everyone in the office." Suddenly, my anesthetized mind came out of its trance, I blinked, my jaw dropped open in awe, and I asked in wonderment, "What did you just say?"

To my amazement, I had heard right the first time. This young, lovely, all-American female—the archetypal girl next door—had just uttered to her employer, whom she barely knew, a vulgar remark that I previously had heard only from truck drivers, construction workers, and attorneys. My response was in the tradition of the late Vince Lombardi. I immediately traded this unrefined woman-child to the Atlanta Falcons for a "go-for," a used IBM Selectric typewriter, and a box of felt-tipped pens. Other than that, all it took was a smile, a severance check, and a good-luck wish. This young woman is free to say the same thing to any other employer if she so desires—and, in turn, that employer is also free to write her a severance check (although in our current decadent lawmaking era, that admittedly is becoming more difficult to do).

All this, however, is a huge plus for you. The fact that we live in a society infested with rudeness and bad taste practically guarantees that a little action such as displaying good manners will win you the hearts and pocketbooks of prospects and clients. Simple, mannerly habits like saying "thank you" and "please" are mentally noted by others, especially by those who themselves display good manners. And the people most likely to add value to your life are those who are refined and who appreciate refinement in others. When it comes to good human relations, refinement is another hefty insurance policy for success. It's a habit that may not be important to everyone, but it will never offend anyone.

## Responsibility

There's nothing more irritating than having to deal with a chronological adult whose responsibility level is equivalent to that of a twelve-year-old. There are many ways in which a person can act irresponsibly, but for our purposes I'm referring to irresponsibility as it relates to commitments. In the broadest of terms, the key to being a responsible person is found in the answer to a simple question: Do you do what you say you're going to do? This can be as seemingly insignificant as calling people back when you say you're going to, or going through with a business deal once you've verbally agreed to it. (Note: Not returning phone calls is ungracious; not calling someone when you've committed to do so is irresponsible.)

As you can see, there's a bit of moral overlap here, because, in the purest sense of the word, it's also dishonest not to do what you've told someone you're going to do. But even if you don't agree with the moral aspect, there's no question that the practice of keeping your commitments is pragmatic. As with people not returning phone calls, I refuse to deal with someone once he's failed to keep a commitment, whether it's getting a package of materials to me by a certain date or failing to show up for a meeting. The only exception to this policy is if (1) the person calls me—preferably in advance—and explains why he was (or is) not able to perform as promised, and (2) it's my first such negative experience with him.

The key to keeping your commitments is to be careful about *making* commitments. Better to have someone unhappy about your refusal to commit than angry over your failure to execute. Word travels fast when it comes to responsibility, so pay close attention to your performance in this area. Being responsible is a simple habit to practice, and one you can count on to pay big dividends if you adhere to it on a consistent basis.

## Self-Sufficiency

Self-sufficiency is a trait that evokes admiration from others, which results in people wanting to do business with you. The person with an expansive mental paradigm is likely to be self-sufficient, because his resourcefulness gives him the capacity to find alternative solutions rather than appeal to others for help.

Unfortunately, the first thing most people think of when confronted with an obstacle is to ask for assistance, and, as soon as that happens, their posture is diminished. When you ask someone for a favor, you should understand that you're incurring a debt. It may not be verbally stated, but it's there—in the accounts-receivable section of the other person's Favors Book— just as surely as if you had signed a promissory note. This in turn brings about two negatives:

First, because you have a limited credit line with every person with whom you come in contact, you have to be careful not to use up valuable credit on situations that aren't truly important. The prudent individual always saves some credit for a rainy day. Second, if the accounts-payable section of *your* Favors Book becomes too great, you're likely to find yourself making more and more decisions that others want you to make, and that spells lack of freedom.

Even if you work for someone else, the more you make it a habit to act on your own initiative, to take action without waiting for others to guide you, the more likely you are to get ahead. I like the way Peter Ueberroth, former commissioner of baseball, put it when he said, "Authority is 20 percent given and 80 percent taken."

## Tactfulness

The first step toward being tactful is to nurture the habit of erasing negative and abrasive words and phrases from your vocabulary. You create obstacles to getting the results you want when you use phrases like, "There's one *problem* that has to be resolved first"; "There's *no negotiation* on that point"; "You're *wrong*"; "*I don't care* whether you like it or not"; or, "That's a *lie*." Good human relations require that you employ much more tact than this when it comes to language, such as, "There's only one *issue* that needs to be resolved, and *I don't see any problem with being able to accomplish that*"; "*You could be right,* but I'd like to review the facts one more time"; "*I certainly want you to feel good about this deal,* but let me explain why I think this is the best way to handle it"; or, "*That may be true,* but I'd still like to present the facts as I see them."

The first sampling of phrases could be the basis for a book entitled *How to Lose Friends and Infuriate People.* The second sampling is the basis for superior human relations, and is infinitely more likely to lead to positive results.

The more you directly challenge the words or actions of another party, the less likely you are to get what you're after. I once attended a meeting in New York, the purported purpose of which was to resolve some differences that I and another party had been having with several principals in a partnership with which we were dealing. One of the partners had signed an agreement with us that the other partners maintained was not legally binding. After thoroughly researching the law, we were convinced they had no legal grounds to stand on, but pragmatism motivated us to try to work amiably with them to arrive at an acceptable compromise.

Shortly after we arrived at the office of one of the partners, we sat down at his conference table, and, to our surprise, his first words, delivered in an extremely hostile tone, were, "All right, let's not beat around the bush. Before we even agree to discuss the terms of a possible new deal, you either sign a rescission of the original agreement or we march down to the courthouse and start litigation."

Yikes! It was Muammar Qaddafi in a dress shirt and silk suit. After privately pondering a number of solutions to the surprise dilemma we faced—such as firebombing Muammar's office or pouring a bottle of Liquid Paper on his wig—I decided to fight ignorance with intelligent tact and began the long journey toward a civilized meeting by saturating the air with congenial words. Ultimately, we succeeded in overcoming the gauche behavior of our Hitlerian host and managed to work out an amiable solution to the problem.

Why in the world would anyone who was in a negotiating position of weakness begin a meeting by throwing verbal punches? It could have been the age-old strategy of attacking when you know you're in the wrong or when your posture is weak, hoping that it will throw the other side off balance; or it could have been a case of ego overriding pragmatism; or it could have been nothing more than abject ignorance. Regardless of the reason, it's amateurish and imprudent to come out swinging. When it comes to negotiating, diplomacy and a pair of deuces beat hostility and four aces every time.

A tactful individual also makes it a habit to avoid challenging people, even if he feels sure they're wrong. If it isn't something really crucial, pragmatism dictates that you let it slide. The cost of proving you're right can often be too high, especially if the provee is a customer or a superior. The immediate gratification of flaunting the fact that you were right can prove to be fatal in the long term. At a minimum, the cost of proving you're right usually results in a loss of allies. It's the proverbial case of winning the battle but losing the war.

## Tolerance

Tolerance is one of the most difficult human relations habits to master, because it requires looking past our own beliefs and perceptions and respecting another's right to embrace different beliefs and perceptions. It doesn't mean that we have to agree with the other person, just that we grant him the right to be. Though we're all guilty of intolerance to one degree or another, carried to an extreme it's a surefire way to undercut human relations. Intolerant individuals often display open contempt for people and things that don't fit within the guidelines of their thinking patterns. Bigotry is the end station of the Intolerance Express.

One of the keys to nurturing the habit of tolerance is to simultaneously cultivate the habit of flexibility. Being flexible can make your journey through life much easier, and far more enjoyable, than if your view of the world is rigid. Only zealots and those living through the Age of Infinite Wisdom are totally inflexible. When you're a child, it seems as if everything is black and white. Then when you're twenty-five, things start to become a little gray; at thirty, they become grayer still; finally, at about forty, you feel as though you're looking at the whole world through Los Angeles smog.

The reality is that it's an anti–Ayn Rand world. I was one of the last holdouts when it came to Ayn Rand's inflexible view of the world, a view she expressed so eloquently in such best-selling novels as *Atlas Shrugged* and *The Fountainhead*. I was like one of those World War II Japanese soldiers they find hiding in the mountains in the Philippines every ten years or so—the guy who peeks out of the bushes and asks, in a shaky voice, "Is it over yet?"

After years of being certain that every word Ayn Rand wrote was unequivocally right, I woke up one morning and realized that I was covered with bumps and bruises. Why? Because I had been living through something called *real life*. Repeatedly I would go back and reread *Atlas Shrugged* and *The Fountainhead* to try to figure out what was wrong, until one day I finally said to myself, "Hey, this is great stuff! And if I ever move to another planet that's full of Henry Reardens and Howard Roarks and Dagny Taggarts (fictional characters from Ayn Rand's novels), it's going to be fantastic. But the problem is, I'm not on another planet right now! This is planet Earth, and there are no Dagny Taggarts or Howard Roarks on this planet. The closest we ever came was Gary Cooper."

A onetime close confidant of Ayn Rand's once told me, "Do you know what Ayn Rand's problem was? She thought you were mentally deranged if you dared to disagree with one percent of her philosophy." Ayn Rand's inflexible, intolerant attitude was evident to anyone who closely followed her career. I admired Ayn Rand as a master thinker, and it saddened me to see her die an obviously unhappy, lonely woman. She seemingly felt it was necessary to mold the world in her own image in order to be content. How would you like *your* happiness to depend upon *your* ability to mold the world in *your* image? Talk about a tough occupation, try going into that business sometime. That's what's known as masochistic intolerance.

To help develop the habit of tolerance, when a person makes a mistake, or offends you, or acts in ways that are not to your liking, remind yourself that you don't know what happened to him before he left home this morning, let alone the inside story of his entire life. Behind the face of every human being, deep within the recesses of his gray matter, is a Hollywood tale to be told. Each and every one of us carries our own secret, heavy burdens through life, and those burdens directly impact our actions. It's the height of good human relations to take this reality into consideration when dealing with others.

## Value for Value

The concept of value for value is the foundation for all sound, harmonious human relationships. Value for value is another way of saying "win-win." Tragically, surveys consistently reveal that most people believe that success comes only at the expense of others. In today's age of envy, it's hard for the average person to grasp the principle that the surest way to succeed is to make certain that all parties to a transaction come out ahead.

As with all sound moral principles, making a habit of thinking value for value is also pragmatic. You rest so much better at night if you don't have to depend upon the gratitude of others for your just rewards. In fact, practicing the concept of value for value is the surest way to protect yourself in a business relationship. You can spend a fortune on legal fees and draw up a contract two feet thick, but the reality is that if you manipulate a situation in such a way that it ends up being an onerous deal for the other party, you'll only succeed in buying yourself a lawsuit. **Real-World Rule No. 322: Regardless of what a contract says, no one will get up every morning and go to work for nothing, especially if one or more other parties to a venture are profiting from it.**

Value for value is the antithesis of force. Force always loses in the real world, as evidenced by the fates of political dictators around the globe, from Adolph Hitler to Idi Amin to Ferdinand Marcos. Both Nature and the human will tenaciously resist force. The hopelessness of using force as a means of achieving cooperation can be witnessed in all areas of business. For example, to the extent an employer utilizes force against employees, not only will they resist him and find creative ways to defy his iron-fisted approach, but, like the proverbial rats abandoning a sinking ship, they will turn on him and/or desert him when his business hits the skids. Abraham Lincoln stated it both accurately and succinctly when he said, "Force is all-conquering, but its victories are short-lived." Force is not in harmony with Nature; actions based on value for value are.

Once you develop the habit of thinking in terms of value for value, you'll find it's quite easy to make money. All you need to do is abide by the following value-for-value rules:

First, if you want more, make yourself worth more.

Second, concentrate on quality and service first, and profit will follow as a natural result.

Third, always give more than you expect to get in return.

With respect to number two, when I was in my late teens I operated a fruit stand in the summer months. My father, the most go-the-extra-mile, customer-oriented human being I've ever known, once noticed that I was busy trying to make my fruit displays perfect while a customer patiently stood by and waited for me to finish. After the customer left, my father severely chastised me for my indifference toward the customer, and told me two things that I never forgot: First, when a customer comes in, stop whatever you're doing and give him *all* your attention. Second, *never* argue with a customer, no matter how irrational his statements may be. In the world of business, my father emphasized, the definition of a customer is someone who wants to buy what you're selling, and who therefore is incapable of being wrong.

This brings us to today's world of laziness, incompetence, negligence, and ignorance. How lucky you are that *you* have the right attitude, or at least (hopefully) have made a commitment to develop the right attitude. Since so few people have a customer-oriented attitude, the competition is slim. Imagine how difficult it would have been to succeed during an age when a majority of people were service-oriented.

The attitude of an employee toward his employer, as well as the attitude of all representatives of a business toward its customers, should be "How may I be of the greatest service to you?" This kind of refreshing attitude may sound anachronistic, but it virtually guarantees success. In other words, the fact that most people *don't* operate in this manner is to your great advantage if you do. Every time you run into rudeness, inconvenience, poor service, or indifference toward customers, you're witnessing a business that is actively inviting competition. On the other hand, if *you* maintain the habit of being customer-oriented, you can virtually eliminate competition.

The practice of being customer-oriented is so critically important to success that before leaving the subject of value for value, I'd like to pass along a couple of personal experiences to drive the point home.

## THE DELI DUMMY

If you'd like to go into the deli business, I can almost guarantee you success if you open your deli within a mile of my house. There's a deli near me that has pretty good food, and my wife and I frequented it several times a week for about a year. We usually picked up sandwiches to go, and because we saw the owner so often, we developed an amiable relationship with him. One day we went in to order some sandwiches, and a new girl, perhaps eighteen years old, took our order. Not having a lot of confidence in either deli order-takers or eighteen-year-old girls, I emphasized to her that the order was "to go."

To set the stage, I remind you that we're living in the latter part of the twentieth century, an era in which store clerks and waiters have absolutely no interest in your desires or satisfaction. A majority of the time they're daydreaming about tonight's episode of "Entertainment Tonight," an upcoming rock concert, or last night's wild party. My awareness of this reality compels me to repeat things like "to go" five or ten times when talking to a clerk (to his considerable irritation), though in the end he usually manages to get the order wrong anyway (sometimes, I suspect, on purpose).

So when the eighteen-year-old waitress, Ms. Snippit, handed us our orders on paper plates, I reminded her, in a pleasant tone, "Uh, I said the order was to go." To which she quickly snapped back, "No you didn't." Again, thoughts of firebombing and Liquid Paper flashed through my mind, but my superior tact prevailed. Just then the owner happened to walk by, and I told him that I would appreciate it if he would tell Ms. Snippit to try to keep her lips tightly sealed and pack up our order, whereupon she again lashed out, "He *didn't* tell me the order was to go."

By now, of course, I was wondering how I could have managed to get myself into such a silly situation, so in order to put the matter to rest once and for all, I said to the owner, in a soft, friendly voice, "It's okay, no problem. Just have her wrap the order to go. But you really should explain to this young lady that the customer is always right."

This undoubtedly would have been the end of the matter, but I had forgotten that the deli owner was originally from New York! With a thundering fury, he responded, "The customer is *not* always right. The customer is *not* always right. I can always find plenty of customers, but I can't find decent employees." As you can well imagine, Ms. Snippit, having had her eighteen-year-old view of the world vindicated, immediately flashed an ear-to-ear grin. Whereupon a fascinating question rumbled through my mind: If this deli dummy talks this way to his *best* customers, how does he treat his *worst* customers? Does he throw spoiled liverwurst at them?

If you're really bright, you might have guessed that neither I nor my wife ever returned to the deli. In addition, later that day I happened to mention what had transpired to a friend of mine, who also was a longtime customer of the deli. He replied, "Thanks for telling me; I'll never go back there, either. I can't stand that kind of attitude toward customers." Question: How many *other* customers do you think the deli owner has lost as a result of his "the customer is not always right" attitude? Why in the world would a business owner take such a self-destructive attitude toward his lifeblood? Who knows? Maybe he's insane; or just plain stupid; or simply mad at the world. Regardless, the customer *doesn't care;* customers are totally self-centered. They want only to know what *you* can do for *them*—better, faster, and less expensively. If your life's purpose is to enhance the self-esteem of eighteen-year-old girls, best you stay out of the business world and open a prep school specializing in Disrespect 401.

## Ms. Snippit II

It must not have been my week, because a few days after the deli experience, I stopped in to pick up my laser printer at a computer store where I had taken it to be repaired. Would you believe that the jivy young lass behind the counter appeared to be eighteenish? I gave her my repair receipt, whereupon she called a serviceman to bring my printer to the front counter. So far, no problem. Hold it, though, my paper tray was missing. When I called this to Ms. Snippit II's attention, she snapped back, "You didn't bring in a paper tray with your printer. I know, because I handled the order."

I didn't know whether to order a salami on rye or just start chewing on my printer. "No," I said with a smile. "I know I brought it in, because I thought about it ahead of time and decided I had better bring it just in case the service department needed it."

"And I know you *didn't*," she retorted with a sneer, "because I would have remembered."

Now I had a serious problem on my hands, because everyone knows that the memories of eighteen-year-olds are infallible. The serviceman invited me to go into in the back room with him so we could see if the missing tray had been inadvertently left lying around. Ms. Snippit II followed close behind, intent on protecting her vested interest in the outcome. Unfortunately, there was no extra tray to be found. There were plenty of paper trays, but they all were inserted in other printers. Throughout the search, Ms. Snippit II, in a nose-thumbing tone, kept repeating, "I *told* you that you didn't bring in a paper tray."

As I gently straight-armed Ms. Snippit II, I said to the serviceman, "Look, I don't want to be difficult, but the bottom line is that I *did* bring in my paper tray, and, though I hate to put it this way, I expect to go home with a paper tray, regardless of what you have to do to get me one." Over the near-violent objections of Ms. Snippit II, the serviceman obliged me by taking a tray from another printer, whereupon I made my exit, with the back of my neck burning from the flames shooting out of Ms. Snippit II's nostrils.

Concerned that perhaps I had gone mad (What if I really *didn't* say "to go" five or ten times at the deli, and what if I really *didn't* bring in my paper tray?), when I got home I thoroughly searched my house for the missing paper tray. No luck. However, because the serviceman had been so gracious to me, I took the trouble to call him the next day to let him know that I definitely did not have the other paper tray at my house. Before I could finish, he interrupted me and said, "Oh, just after you left, I found your tray. It was on a top shelf. Sorry for the inconvenience."

I don't know, maybe it's just something about minimum-wage eighteen-year-olds. . . .

Now, some people might be inclined to say that it's not the owner of the computer store who's at fault, that perhaps *he* thinks in terms of value-for-value service even if his employees don't. Hogwash! The owner who cares enough about his customers not only will take the trouble to instill his business philosophy in his employees, he'll also make certain that they *follow through* on his policies. When it comes to bad service, it's *always* the owner's fault.

## The Great Catalyst

In this chapter, I've tried to touch on as many good human relations traits as was feasible, but there's no limit to the number of ways in which you can improve your ability to obtain and retain the goodwill of others. There is no way to escape the reality that you have to deal with other people in order to succeed to any meaningful degree. Nor is there any escaping the reality that the more successful you are in getting others to cooperate with you, the easier it becomes to reach your goals.

No matter how much knowledge you have about your business or profession, you'll always fall short of your aim if you fail to practice sound human relations habits.

No one ever becomes perfect at this art, but the good news is that it's within your power to improve at it every day of your life. And the better you become, the more you will attract others who possess a sincere appreciation for superior human relations. Remember, when you practice the Human Relations Habit you attract attractive human beings, and attractive human beings add value to your life. There is no better catalyst for getting results than gaining the goodwill of others.

If you already knew everything about human relations discussed in this chapter, all you have to do now is put your knowledge into practice on a consistent basis. When you do so, you'll be pleased to find that it's like running a race with the wind at your back, with everything that you want out of life as the prize.

# Chapter 7

# The Simplicity Habit

If it's true that we teach best those things we need to learn, I should be at my finest in this chapter. For as long as I can remember, I've carried on a ferocious battle against my obsessive-compulsive instincts in an effort to simplify my life. I used to think it was a sickness unique to me, but I've come to realize that everyone, to one degree or another, wrestles with the problem of trying to uncomplicate his life.

It's amazing how cavalierly we dissipate our most precious resource—time—by complicating our lives. Given a choice between doing something in a simple or complex manner, most people will tend to choose the complex route. Why? If I knew, I wouldn't have spent so many years redrafting letters four or five times and organizing my desk and filing systems to perfection. Maybe human beings just love pain.

Whatever the reasons, experience has convinced me that, all other things being equal, simplicity is almost always the best approach when it comes to getting results. Over the past decade, I've begun to experience the delicious effects of simplicity, and I'm now perplexed about how I found so many ways to complicate my life in bygone years. What a cathartic feeling to rid oneself of thoughts, projects, and activities that clutter both one's mind and life, while contributing little or nothing to the achievement of one's goals.

It's impossible to place a value on a clear mind, because when you cleanse your cranial computer of the thousands of trivial thoughts that continually bombard it, it makes it possible for you to concentrate on thoughts that have the potential to make a real difference in your life.

Most of us are drowning in a sea of unimportant to marginally important papers. I long ago concluded that the reason I kept tens of thousands of letters, notes, contracts, memos, and other papers neatly filed away and meticulously indexed is because I feared that I might someday have to prove a point to someone. The problem, however, was that eventually I reached a point of diminishing returns: I ended up with so much paper that I had difficulty finding the documents that really *were* important.

Years of experience convinced me that only a tiny fraction of all the papers I saved ever were needed. Even when they were, I found that the consequences of not being able to find a document (the document you need is almost always the one you can't find) were never as grim as I had imagined. It was a losing proposition from every aspect. It makes one take seriously Buddha's observation that "all unhappiness is caused by attachment."

## Overcommitment

In the previous chapter, I told you how I used to have a problem giving someone a firm and immediate *no* if I didn't want to go along with something that was requested of me. I also stated that the key to keeping your commitments is to be careful about making commitments. The only thing worse than not saying *no* immediately is to say *yes* immediately. If you're too generous or too fast on the trigger with your *yes*'s, it's likely to result in endless frustration and an unnecessarily complicated life. In my second book, *Looking Out For #1*, I offered a simple antidote to this universal problem, and it's still the best one I know of:

*Learn to say no politely and pleasantly, but immediately and firmly.* This is a remarkably easy-to-master habit that can dramatically simplify your life.

It's hard enough to avoid spreading yourself too thin just keeping up with the things you absolutely have to do and want to do—such as working, sleeping, exercising, reading, spending time with your family, and enjoying various kinds of recreation —without committing to an excess of marginal projects in a hopeless effort to accommodate everyone. **Real-World Rule No. 231: Don't be so much to everyone else that you become nothing to yourself.**

## The Penny-Ante Trap

The Penny-Ante Trap is the inability to overlook minor, perceived injustices, especially when they involve money. Remember that even though life doesn't always seem fair, you do have the power to control how you react to its unfairnesses. Don't spend hours—and certainly not days or weeks—trying to rectify a wrong that involves a relatively small amount of money. To keep from complicating your life, it's important to develop the habit of immediately asking yourself if the amount of time you'll have to invest to remedy what you perceive to be an injustice is really worth it. It's a real sucker trap, and the smaller the person's mind, the more likely he is to get caught in it.

A friend recently asked my advice regarding an irritating situation. A rather nasty beauty salon operator had purchased some beauty products from her, only because the wholesaler he normally ordered from had gone out of business. My friend was reluctant to sell to him because she had had problems with him in a couple of earlier encounters. Sure enough, about two months after the salon operator purchased the products from my friend, he called her and, in a hostile tone, demanded that she take back the items he had not sold and immediately issue him a refund. Her company's policy, which was stated on its invoices, was not to accept any returns unless they were made within thirty days of purchase, and then only if the products still were in their original cartons. If these two conditions were met, the customer could then receive a credit toward other purchases. The invoices clearly stated that cash refunds would not be issued under any circumstances.

Not only was the hostile salon operator way past the thirty-day limit for returning merchandise, he also did not have the original cartons. On top of that he was demanding a cash refund. My friend wanted to know what I would do if I were she. I asked her whether she liked the salon operator enough to give him part of her life. "Of course not," she responded.

"Well, if he's as hostile as you claim," I continued, "he'll drain you of an enormous amount of time and energy before the matter is resolved, and, regardless of the outcome, you will have lost that time and energy forever. Since you could care less about him, the only relevant question is, 'How much do you value your own time and energy?' "

It's back to the cost of proving you're right. The purpose of life isn't to see how often you can prove you're right. The purpose of life is to live. When you run into an ugly situation like the one just described, get in the habit of weighing the realities carefully before taking a tough stand. Who needs the aggravation? You should be spending most of your time working on opportunities and creative projects, not penny-ante problems.

## The Dally Dummy

For years it drove me crazy trying to figure out why so many people worked fewer hours than I, yet did much better financially. Then one day I happened to read an article about numerous studies that indicated that the most successful people are not workaholics. What they're good at is achieving the best possible results in the shortest period of time. That one hurt real bad. When I looked in the mirror this time, I saw a real-life Dally Dummy staring back at me. Simply too much dallying—too many paper clips and staples being applied, too many letters being rewritten, too many copies of documents being made, too many labels being neatly affixed—too many details that simply didn't matter.

Since I've become seminormal, I've been fascinated by the reality that very few things in daily life really matter that much; i.e., most things simply don't have the potential to make a significant impact on the quality of a person's life. Now my first objective every day is to completely eliminate as many projects as possible. Hands down, the simplest way to complete any task is to eliminate it. However, it isn't always feasible to discard a project. When that's the case, you should make it a habit to simplify it and get it off your desk as quickly as possible. A little discipline like allowing yourself to handle a piece of paper only once can have a major impact on the quality of your results.

To simplify my life, I've attacked the Dally Dummy within me in many ways, and one of the most important of these is to make it a regular habit to follow the "Three Gets." When I enter my office each morning, I consciously think to myself: "Get in. Get it done. Get out!" It may sound simplistic, but accidentally stapling my tie to a letter as a result of dallying is even more simplistic.

Why do the Three Gets work? Because of the truth inherent in the maxim that work expands to fill the time available for its completion. Once you've mentally absorbed this reality and cultivated the habit of guarding against it, you've practically bought yourself a whole new life.

## The Meeting Trap

Simplicity ends where meetings begin. A Dally Dummy takes to meetings like a play-by-play sports announcer clings to clichés. When someone requests a meeting with you, the first question in your mind should be, "Is this meeting really necessary?" And when someone does convince you that a meeting is necessary, demand that he get to the point. Refuse to allow any meeting to drag on beyond its useful life.

Remember the trade-off: If you're in a meeting, you can't be working on creative projects that have the potential to produce meaningful results. Contrary to a generally accepted but erroneous belief, all the great ideas and discoveries throughout history began as a creative seed planted in the mind of a single individual. John Steinbeck alluded to this in his novel *East of Eden*, when he said, "The group can build and extend [an idea], but the group never invents anything. The preciousness lies in the lonely mind of a man."

## The Plight of the Supernothing

One of the most crucial of all simplicity habits is to concentrate on what you do best and let others do the rest. Remember, the objective is to get results, not see how many aptitudes you can flaunt. Too many aptitudes lead to the emergence of that great Supernothing within each of us, and thus to an unnecessarily complicated life. I'm convinced that this is one of the chief causes of failure.

People often forget that we live in a division-of-labor society in which it not only isn't necessary to do everything yourself, it isn't even necessary to understand how something works to use it. You don't need an intricate knowledge of automobile engines to drive a car. You don't need to understand how television signals are transmitted to use a television set. It usually will cost you a lot more in wasted time *not* to pay for someone else's services and to try to do something yourself that you aren't qualified to do.

This lesson hit me between my right and left forebrain when I bought my first personal computer. Have you ever tried to read a computer manual? I'm absolutely convinced that it's a conspiracy: Those manuals are written in English by Japanese! Day after day I relentlessly studied the manual that came with my computer, trying to suppress my frustration and stubbornly believing that if I just stuck with it, sooner or later I would learn how to turn on the computer!

Finally, just as I was on the verge of being committed to the Computer Institute for Low-Tech Mental Arthritics, the solution struck me. I looked in the Yellow Pages and called a computer instructor who specialized in word processing. I told him that my interest in computers was limited to writing books and outlining speeches, so I was interested only in learning how to use a word-processing program. I also emphasized that I did *not* want to learn anything about computers, per se.

Would you believe that the instructor had me functional on the computer in about an hour, and reasonably proficient by the end of the day? And after the second (and last) lesson, I was breezing. Now I'm so fast it embarrasses me. But I still don't know a thing about computers! Let others be computer experts if that's their objective. My objective is to write books and outline speeches, so for me a computer is only a means to an end.

The point is that any time spent working on projects that don't take advantage of your best talents is time inefficiently used. The common term is *delegation*—parceling out jobs to others, whether those others be employees or outside people whom you pay to do the work. Delegation is absolutely essential to the maintenance of a simple life, and at the heart of good delegation is the willingness to *let go*. For obsessive-compulsives like me, it doesn't get any worse than this. Most people make the mistake of trying to battle their deficiencies; instead, they should hire out their deficiencies and nurture their skills. President Dwight Eisenhower once said, "The mark of a good executive is when you're handed letters that you know you could have written better yourself and you sign them anyway."

Merely telling someone to do something, however, does not constitute effective delegation. Implementing the following steps will go a long way toward helping you to excel at this art:

1. Tell people exactly what you want them to accomplish.

2. Let them be creative and find a way to accomplish it. In other words, don't try to solve your subordinates' problems for them. This means that you have to let go and allow other people to do it their way, at least within a reasonable framework.

3. Spot-check their work on a regular basis.

4. If their work is unsatisfactory, redirect them.

Getting into the habit of delegating pays exponential dividends by simplifying your life and increasing your balance sheet.

## The Crux of the Issue

The late Joe Karbo, author of the much-publicized book *The Lazy Man's Way to Riches*, was fond of saying that most people are too busy earning a living to make any money. What Karbo meant was that the average person never seems to find the time to work on the really important things, the creative projects that produce big payoffs. It is creativity, not hard work, that is at the heart of success in any field of endeavor. And in order for a person to have the time to engage in creative thinking, he must learn to work efficiently.

To do this, it's crucial to develop the habit of focusing on the crux of the issue. By *crux of the issue*, I mean the point or points upon which success or failure rests. You must resist the temptation to get sidetracked by peripheral issues that cannot yield a payoff no matter what their outcome.

In this regard, people often confuse the means with the end. Did you ever grind away at a project for hours, then look up and ask yourself, "Why am I doing this?" More often than not, the reason is that you got caught up in trying to make the details perfect, and in the process lost sight of your original objective. Many people spend most of their time working on details, hopelessly trying to make everything perfect. Unfortunately, in the real world such perfection doesn't produce meaningful results.

To paraphrase Peter Drucker, you should concentrate on doing the right things rather than doing things right. In other words, more important than the question of whether or not you're spending too much time on a project is the question, Should I be working on this project *at all?* Focusing on the crux of the issue requires an understanding of what's important to work on and what isn't.

You're probably familiar with the 80–20 Rule, which states that the average person spends 80 percent of his time on tasks and projects that produce 20 percent of his results. For example, did you ever notice that carelessly typed envelopes and shoddily wrapped packages with messy labels seem to arrive just as quickly as those that look as though they had been produced by Michelangelo? Though it can be a tough reality for a perfectionist to accept, the truth is that the aesthetics of an envelope or package simply don't matter. They have nothing whatsoever to do with the substance of the contents.

A person has a choice: He can spend his time editing commas and wrapping packages, or he can utilize his time working on important, creative projects. The latter produces financial results, the former produces only high blood pressure and twitching. Fighting the 80–20 Rule is an ongoing battle, and to aid me in this battle, years ago I made the following sign and hung it on my office wall:

> **Does it matter?**
> **If so, how *much* does it matter?**

The reason I included the second question on the sign is that you can argue that *everything* matters to one extent or another, and that's true. But the more important question is, How *much* does it matter? It's the habit of asking myself this second question that continually reminds me to focus my energies on the crux of every issue.

Looking at the crux of the issue in the broadest possible

terms, the real question is, What do I need to do right now to achieve maximum positive results in my life? Believe me, you don't have much time for anything else. Understanding this reality has a great deal to do with how hard—and how much— you have to work to get where you want to be in life.

## The Ultimate Simplicity Formula

In 1980, after the publication of my third book, *Restoring the American Dream*, I was contacted by an elderly gentleman named Paul who wanted to buy a large quantity of the book in hardcover. He wanted to start a grass-roots campaign to "change the course of Western Civilization." Several times he invited me to come to his home in Las Vegas, and once I concluded that he was really serious about his intentions (he had already purchased about 5,000 copies of the book), I agreed to make the trip.

My visit to Las Vegas to meet Paul is barely believable, but it really happened. Paul picked me up at the airport, and we drove directly to an empty lot on the outskirts of the city. We then pulled into a driveway that was closed off by iron gates. After we paused for a moment, the electric gates swung open and we proceeded to drive to a vacant area, the most notable feature of which was a cluster of giant-size boulders. Paul then stopped his car near the boulders, at which point I began to wonder what I was getting myself into.

After we got out of the car, Paul approached the boulders, waved his hand, and said aloud, "Open sesame." Just like in the story of Ali Baba, one of the large boulders slowly began to swing open. He had me follow him into a dark hallway inside the pile of boulders, which I (nervously) did. After a few steps, we came to—of all things—an elevator. As I stepped into the elevator, the thought crossed my mind that I might never again be seen alive. I might end up one of those people who mysteriously disappears, with not a trace of evidence left behind.

The elevator descended slowly, and after about twenty seconds came to a gentle stop. The door opened and I found myself in an underground paradise: beautiful landscaping, with trees, bushes, and flowers as authentic-looking as anything I had seen at Disneyland, a majestic home, a freestanding guest house, a rock-formed swimming pool and jacuzzi, and many more wonders beyond anything a humble word hacker like myself could possibly describe.

After a tour of the vast underground grounds, we rested in the sprawling living room of Paul's home and chatted. He said he wanted to buy 70,000 hardcover copies of *Restoring the American Dream*, and, out of the goodness of my heart, I agreed to sell them to him at a discount. (If you're going to become an author, this is the kind of fan you need!) As the conversation unfolded, I inferred that Paul's net worth was in the area of $500 million, which was quite impressive, especially for a mole. I finally asked him, perhaps presumptuously, "Paul, how in the world did you ever accumulate such wealth?"

His answer was the essence of simplicity. He said, "You know, making money really is a very simple proposition. All you do is charge the highest price for your product or service that the market will bear, keep your expenses as low as possible, and in between is your profit."

Whereupon I suavely retorted, "Gaa . . . llee."

Indeed, Paul had never been involved in any kind of complex business or venture. Starting out as a one-man delivery service in the Brooklyn–New Jersey area fifty years earlier (with a used truck he had purchased for $100), he had religiously followed his simple success formula, accumulated huge cash reserves, then continually multiplied his wealth by buying assets for cash, holding on to them until the market demand was sufficiently high, then selling them at substantial profits. (If this sounds familiar, it's because Paul is the same individual I described in Chapter 3, the one who lost his house during the Depression.)

## The Other Side of the Coin

That meeting with Paul really opened my eyes. From that point on, I became conscious of how most people, including myself, unnecessarily complicate the process of making money. In particular, I never forgot the part of Paul's success formula that called for keeping expenses as low as possible. Having won nine consecutive World High-Overhead Titles at a relatively young age, I can tell you that high overhead is one of the easiest ways to complicate your existence.

In my previous life, I developed a reputation as a professional employer. By that I mean I didn't produce a product or service, I just employed people. No matter what my circumstances were at any given time, I kept everyone on the payroll—marketing people, analysts, secretaries, receptionists, assistant receptionists, go-fors. You name the job; if I didn't have it, I'd create it for you. It was my own little welfare state. I managed to keep all my employees busy with make-work projects, which allowed them to continue drawing paychecks during even the worst of times.

It was absolutely great. My employees were able to afford tickets to ball games and concerts, eat at the finest restaurants, and set aside money for vacations—nothing but the best for them. What a contribution I made to society. My employees didn't have to depend on Uncle Sam to take care of them. They had their own personal Uncle Dumb to do the job. Unfortunately, every entrepreneur who has made this noble mistake has found out the hard way that there's one major flaw in the system: The dollars flow in only one direction; no one looks out for Uncle Dumb! Worse, through some remarkable quirk of human nature, gratitude quickly turns to hostility when those payroll checks no longer clear the bank—no matter how generous you were with your employees when the good times were rolling. (If all this causes some bad memories from your own past to resurface, you may want to take a break, retrieve your Employee Doll from the middle drawer of your desk, and brush up on your dart throwing.)

There's a direct correlation between high overhead—and particularly high labor costs—and a complicated business life. Just as it's important to learn the habit of not dwelling on penny-ante matters, so too is it important to practice the habit of keeping overhead to a minimum.

## A Lousy One Percent Profit

Everyone has heard the adage about not trying to reinvent the wheel, but I question how many people really take it to heart. We're living in an age of computers, satellites, and genetic technology, but who was the richest man in America until recently? Sam Walton, of Walmart Stores. And what does Sam Walton do? The same thing that Jewish merchants were doing thousands of years ago in the Middle East and hundreds of years ago in Europe—"buying things for a dollar, selling them for two dollars, and making a lousy one percent profit."

Likewise, Holiday Inns merely adopted Howard Johnson's motel-chain idea and did a better job. White Castle was in business more than twenty years before Ray Kroc came along, but McDonald's borrowed White Castle's hamburger-chain concept and carried it to new heights. IBM was around for decades before Steven Jobs ever thought of Apple Computer. And all Century 21 did was find a new way to organize a business that had been in existence for centuries.

**Real-World Rule No. 101: It's a lot simpler to follow a pioneer than be a pioneer.** The easiest and most direct path to finding a marketable product or service is to modify a known success.

## Minding the Store

Nor do you have to think in terms of rapid expansion to strike it rich. The best example I know of is that of a longtime friend, Fred Hayman. Fred, a native of Switzerland, never finished high school, but managed to secure a job as a management apprentice at the Waldorf-Astoria Hotel in New York not too long after he came to the United States. In 1954 he transferred to Los Angeles, where he worked as a chef at the Beverly Hilton Hotel.

A short time later, Fred bought into a failing clothing store in Beverly Hills. His two partners ultimately wanted to close down the operation and cut their losses, but Fred instead bought them out. By his own admission, he knew nothing at all about the retail business, but he stayed with that one store, nurtured it like a mother hen, pampered his customers like no one ever before had done, and was on the premises every day overseeing (as in delegating) all aspects of his operation.

The store's reputation for quality and service became so well known that, without ever opening a second branch, Giorgio virtually became a household name nationwide. In 1982, capitalizing on the remarkable name identification he had built, Fred launched Giorgio perfume. The fragrance was marketed through prestigious department stores across the country and became an immediate sensation. Five years later, he sold his perfume company to Avon for a tidy $165 million.

Fred Hayman shattered a lot of entrepreneurial myths with his one-store megasuccess. The key lesson is that it's not whether you have one store or a thousand stores, it's your methodology that determines the bottom line. Even Ray Kroc said that initially he never thought about franchising McDonald's, that his main focus was on making his first unit operate as smoothly as possible. He explained that once you have a single operation running efficiently and profitably, nationwide expansion is a relatively simple process.

Most entrepreneurs overemphasize expansion at the outset, failing to take the necessary time and effort to nail down a solid, workable foundation upon which to build. **Real-World Rule No. 208: The more rapid the expansion, particularly in the early years, the less likely a business is to succeed.** A partial corollary: The long-term success of a venture tends to be inversely proportional to the amount of immediate success, or perceived immediate success, of the venture.

Get into the habit of working hard to find simple deals, then find simple ways to profit from them.

## The Complexity of Greener Grass

Another mistake with which I am all too familiar is believing that a fatiguing travel schedule is a key to making money. In truth, it's not necessary to perpetually crisscross the country to find good deals, because there are probably more than you can handle right in your own backyard.

I recall the sad tale of an acquaintance from yesteryear who owned a large home on a prestigious street along the ocean in the Los Angeles area. Herb had been a typical wheeler-dealer builder for many years, continually traveling the country and building monuments to himself in the form of bigger and bigger high-rise office buildings and apartment complexes. I say typical, because in the end, like most high-flying builders, he went belly-up.

Years later we had occasion to discuss his trials and tribulations, and he said to me, "You know, I spent a fortune while enduring all the discomfort and inconvenience associated with traveling to distant cities to develop large projects. It was a never-ending nightmare of hassling with skycaps, ticket agents, stewardesses, taxi drivers, and bellmen, checking in and out of hotels, and all the other horrors that go with business travel, and it turned out to be all for nothing.

"What's so ironic about it is that if I had just stayed home all those years and taken a one-hour walk up and down my own street every day, keeping an eye open for properties that were for sale, I could have made millions with very little effort. All I would have needed to do was buy up virtually every property that came on the market. During the years I was wheeling and dealing all over the country, the real estate on my own street increased in value ten times or more."

In relating this story to you, I'm not suggesting that there isn't money to be made in distant cities. What I am saying is that, all other things being equal, you should try the simplest path first: Carefully check out the deals in your own backyard before venturing cross-country in search of that ever-elusive greener grass.

## Make It Easy on Yourself

In the first chapter I alluded to a marketing maxim that says, If you want to do well, sell people what they need; if you want to get rich, sell people what they want. However, I should caution you that if you try to sell people what you think they need, you may not even do well. You may, in fact, go broke in the process. The problem with selling people what you think they need—even if they really need it—is that it takes too long and costs too much to educate them, i.e., to convince them that they need your product or service.

Probably to a more exaggerated extent than at any time in recorded history, people today demand instant gratification. Government policies during the last half of this century have convinced the average citizen that he has a *right* to whatever he wants—and he has a right to it *now*. New cars, homes, vacations, video recorders, and expensive, frivolous trinkets are now rights to the average person. If you try to buck this reality and insist on trying to sell people what you believe they need, you're hopelessly complicating the process of making money.

The simplest, safest approach to financial success is to be an accommodating free-enterpriser and make it a habit to sell people what they *want*.

## The Thrill of Coercion

Anyone who bothers to read the newspaper cannot help but notice the proliferation of business regulations, fines, and imprisonment of white-collar types during the past decade. It should be clear to all but the most naïve or uninformed individual that one of the best ways to complicate your financial life is to become involved in an industry highly regulated by government bureaucrats (aka City Business Poachers, State Business Poachers, and Federal Business Poachers).

The government doesn't restrict itself to the excitement of frying Big Fish, either. It's true that when a Michael Milken comes along and has the gall to violate the most sacred of all federal laws—Thou Shalt Not Make Enormous Sums of Money—agency chiefs and prosecutors begin salivating and riling the masses by giving daily media interviews on the evils of wealth (until such time, of course, as they themselves receive lucrative offers to join one of the prestigious law firms that defends the "evil" people they are trying to prosecute). Today, however, *everyone* is fair game. All you need to do is attract attention, and the easiest way to attract attention is to be in a highly regulated business.

I used to jog occasionally with an attorney who previously had been a federal prosecutor. During one early morning jog he told me, "Robert, you just can't imagine the thrill of having the full force of the federal government behind you. Coercing people becomes a way of life; it's addictive. All of us young prosecutors used to compare notes and joke about our most recent extortion triumphs. People either caved in to our demands or lived to regret it. It was absolutely intoxicating."

Forget about whether or not you think it's fair. Right and wrong simply aren't relevant when it comes to government interference. What I'm talking about here is reality. The important thing is to understand that if you want to simplify your pursuit of wealth, you should stay as far away from the Business Poachers as possible.

## Knowing Your Principals

You can also save precious time, and simplify your life in the process, by being realistic about the principals with whom you deal. There are two kinds of principals, in particular, who can turn your business pursuits into living nightmares.

The first of these is the principal who is not highly motivated. It's tough enough to close a deal when all the parties involved are enthusiastic, but when motivation is low on the part of one or more of the key principals, complications are almost always close at hand. If a principal isn't motivated, the two most likely outcomes are: (1) He will ultimately back out of the deal, regardless of how many times he may have agreed to it, or (2) sensing that he's in the driver's seat, he will repeatedly attempt to negotiate a better deal for himself.

The second kind of principal who is a menace to simplicity is someone who doesn't have the final authority to make key decisions. If you're not talking directly with the person who can say *yes* or *no*, it's wise to take everything, especially assurances, with a grain of salt. Better still, work on a different deal, one in which you have direct access to the decision maker.

Cultivating the habit of being realistic about the principals with whom you deal is a huge step toward simplifying your deal-making pursuits.

## Ga-Ga Land

Finally, be careful about deals that are contingent upon some further major activity taking place, especially any kind of exotic financing, such as the ever-elusive, mysterious "offshore funding"—a phenomenon that I've never once seen materialize in all my years of deal making. Contingencies have a remarkable way of never coming to fruition.

Nowhere is the primrose path of contingencies more crowded than in Ga-Ga Land—also known as the world of real estate developers. If you're a real estate agent who has a commission at stake, it's always safest to assume that there *is no second phase*. Remember, tomorrow is a promissory note, but today is cash. **Real-World Rule No. 94: In the world of real estate developers, the second phase is something called *bankruptcy*.** Do yourself a favor and simplify your life by following the simple habit of steering clear of contingencies.

## The Joy of Simplicity

There are more ways to complicate your life, both business and personal, than there are pages in this book, so the best overall guide I can offer is to urge you to cultivate the habits of using common sense and not deluding yourself. Discard the notion, once and for all, that it's necessary to make things complex in order to make money.

Simplicity grants you a great deal of freedom, and freedom is perhaps the most positive result you can achieve. Take it from someone who was imprisoned by complexities throughout much of his life. As I said at the outset of this chapter, if simplifying your life has been a problem for you, you're not alone. Virtually everyone possesses the problem to one degree or another, so you should resign yourself to the fact that it takes a lot of hard work.

It's worth repeating: It's the freest feeling in the world to rid yourself of projects and activities that clutter your life and contribute little or nothing to the achievement of your goals. You should be spending most of your time concentrating on constructive projects and activities that have the potential to make a real difference in the quality of your life.

To get where you want to be on the success ladder, in the shortest possible period of time, it pays to put a great amount of effort into making the Simplicity Habit a central theme of your daily life.

# Chapter 8

# The Drain People Elimination Habit

Drain People are people who drain you of time, energy, peace of mind, relaxation, comfort, and/or money. Unfortunately, there are no statutes on the books outlawing the actions of Drain People. The only defense against them is for you to keep them, and/or get them, out of your life.

As a now-forgotten student of human nature once pointed out, you'll never smell like a rose if you roll in a dunghill. No matter what else you do right, if you associate with the wrong people, it's virtually impossible to succeed. In addition to causing endless complications, Drain People make you look bad in the eyes of others because of the generally accepted truth in the adage that "birds of a feather flock together." Whom you associate with is like a neon sign that tells the world where you are on the success ladder at any given point in time.

Eliminating Drain People from your life can be a difficult task. One reason for this is that sidestepping a persistent Drain Person can cause significant discomfort. Another is that even when you know someone is a Drain Person, it's often tempting to make an exception for short-term profit. This is known as: Major Mistake. Trust me, you can't afford the long-term cost of the exception.

Finally, human beings have a tendency to give others the

benefit of the doubt. People often make remarks like, "But he means well." Maybe I'm dense, but I don't understand how to interpret "means well." I know what high blood pressure is. I know what a headache is. I know what aggravation is. But I'm not sure what "means well" is. Does it mean that someone should be allowed to rob you of time, energy, and happiness because you think his intentions are good?

You don't have enough hours in your life to give proper attention to the people you already know to be worthy, so why stretch your boundaries to find new ones? It's far better to trust your instincts and err on the side of caution. With each passing year, my instincts about people continue to improve, and undoubtedly you've found the same to be true of yours. **Real-World Rule No. 155: The most prudent guideline to follow for judging potential Drain People is: When in doubt, keep them out!**

Finally, don't make the often-fatal error of believing that a Drain Person will change, and certainly don't engage in any attempt to change him. People rarely, if ever, change—a lesson I've had to learn repeatedly. I recall one party many years ago who so offended me with his deceit and treachery in a business deal that I decided to strike him completely from my life, going to the extreme of cutting off all communication with him. I reasoned that if he could stoop to such a low level of integrity once, it must be so ingrained in his personality that he would not hesitate to do it again if the opportunity were to present itself.

To this terminally dishonest person's credit, he did send several letters of apology over the years. Finally, I relented and not only opened the lines of communication once more, but, over a period of time, began discussing a number of business proposals with him. The gory details of the story make me blush, so I'll get to the bottom line: After a brief period of time, he proved, as you've probably already guessed, that the first time around was no accident—that he was an individual who was capable of rising to incomprehensible levels of insincerity. Not only did he again display his lack of character at the moment of truth, he even managed to outdo his earlier reprehensible deeds. This little anecdote may have reminded you of a similar experience from your own past, because most of us take the same classes (though not necessarily in the same order) during our enrollment at the University of Life.

What I've just described illustrates the Law of the Scorpion, which is based on a tale you may have heard before.

A scorpion sitting at the edge of a pond spots a frog. He asks the frog, "Hey, pal, how about giving me a lift to the other side of the pond? I can't swim."

The frog replies, "You've got to be kidding. No way I'm that dumb. I know what you guys are like. If I let you get on my back, you'll sting me, and I'll drown. Forget it."

The scorpion persists. "I can't believe how stupid you are. If I'm on your back, why in the world would I sting you when I can't swim? If you drown, I'll drown, too."

"Hmm, good point," reasons the frog. "Okay, get on."

The scorpion hops on the frog's back, and the frog takes off for the other side of the pond. About halfway across, sure enough, the scorpion lets the frog have a gigantic, poisonous sting in his back, and the two of them start to go under. With his last dying breath, the frog asks the scorpion, "Why in the heck did you do that? Now we're both going to drown."

To which the scorpion replies, with *his* last dying breath, "I couldn't help it. It's my nature."

Moral: Once a Drain Person, always a Drain Person; it's his nature. As an ancient proverb warns us, You must have gold to make gold. Simplify your life by not deluding yourself into believing that a Drain Person will change. Once a person begins to drain you, cut your losses short and get him completely out of your life. **Real-World Rule No. 42: Never leave the door open after a small evil manages to make its way inside, because only greater evils are waiting to gain entrance.** Bad character is malignant; it grows and spreads if not checked early on.

# Roll Call

Following are some examples of Drain People that you've probably encountered at one time or another. An all-inclusive list could fill several volumes, but this sampling is more than adequate for our purposes. My objective is to jog your memory to perhaps bring to mind a Drain Person or two you may have unthinkingly allowed to slip into your life and remain there unchallenged. Even if the culprit doesn't fall into one of the categories below, my review hopefully will succeed in flushing him from your subconscious and into the open where you can more thoroughly and objectively examine him. If you aspire to great success, you absolutely must breed the habit of eliminating Drain People from your life.

## The Burr Person

Professional speakers, in particular, are all too familiar with the Burr Person, the individual who since birth has had a burr firmly stuck in a sensitive part of his anatomy, and acts accordingly. At speeches and seminars, he sits stiffly in his seat, arms folded in front of him, scowl chiseled on his face, and a sign rubber-stamped across his forehead that challenges the speaker: "Impress me."

Forget it, you can't. A Burr Person has made up his mind ahead of time; the permanency of his burr problem guarantees that. This is the kind of individual who subscribes to everything and orders every kind of direct-mail trinket imaginable. Then, after he has had sufficient time to read and use everything he ordered, he cancels all his subscriptions and returns all the adult mail-order toys he bought. But that's only the beginning. Two days after canceling the subscription or returning the merchandise, he contacts the Postmaster General, the Federal Trade Commission, the local district attorney, the FBI, and the Commander of NATO, screaming to them that he has been defrauded, and demanding immediate justice. Even government bureaucrats don't take him seriously, which is saying a lot.

All the regulatory agencies have developed form letters for the Burr Person, and routinely send copies to the appropriate parties as the complaints roll in.

Burr People are everywhere, and they're particularly noted for their lack of humor. Nothing irritates them more than being around people who are happy or who are on a motivational roll. I recall one particular Burr Person from my previous life who, listening to me excitedly describe how positive I felt about life, glowered at me and said, in an irritated voice, "I don't see why everything has to be positive. What's *wrong* with being negative?" What a perfectly delightful point of view.

Be humane to the Burr Person by maintaining the habit of keeping your smiling face out of his sight so he can be angry to his heart's content.

## The Changer

The Changer doesn't deal in money; he deals in (attempted) people change. Specifically, he wants to change *you*. The Changer cannot be happy unless he is successful in converting you to his ways. While continually chastising you for not changing, it never occurs to him that you may not *want* to change, that you're actually happy with your life the way it is. And certainly it never crosses his mind that you find *his* way of life deplorable.

## The Chiseler

The Chiseler is a world-class drainer. In fact, he counts on wearing you down so he eventually can get his way. Nothing can be smooth or simple with him. The Chiseler always has to get a better deal, an extra bonus, a larger cut. The ultimate is when it comes time for him to write you a check. Never mind that he owes you the money, he practically makes you beg for it. There's a bit of sadism in every world-class Chiseler.

Unless you're a fellow Chiseler who enjoys a good chisel match now and then with one of your own kind, the Chiseler is truly repugnant. He's really nothing more than a scorpion in a business suit. It's simply not possible for him to change; it's his nature.

## The Conditional Person

The Conditional Person roams the earth bearing strings-attached gifts for the unwary. His game is entrapment. He needs to give to others so he can turn around and pounce on his prey, demanding (usually in subtle ways) to extract a psychological price equal to what he perceives to be the value of his gift—plus, of course, 385 percent compounded interest. Nothing makes a Conditional Person happier than bumping into a naïve taker. Beware of Conditional People bearing gifts of incense and myrrh, especially if they want you to sign a promissory note.

## The Deal Gabber

Did you ever talk to someone about a deal and be delighted to find that he's very excited about it, often so excited that he urges you to send him the pertinent information via Federal Express? When you're dealing with a Deal Gabber, a most amazing thing then happens: nothing. After not hearing from him for two days, you call his office, only to find that he's on vacation for two weeks and that he left on the very day he told you to Fed Ex the material to him. So why did he urge you to send the information to him Fed Ex? Nothing mysterious about it: Deal Gabbers simply love to gab.

Every phase of one's life must ultimately come to an end, and so it was that after 11,287 Deal Gabber experiences, the Deal Gabber phase of my life ended on an all-time, super-duper Deal Gabber episode. After discussing a certain deal with a (then unknown to me) Deal Gabber named Charles, and taking great pains to qualify his degree of interest, he asked me to send the pertinent information to him by Federal Express. He pointed out that since it was Friday I should send it to his home for Saturday delivery because he was leaving town on Monday. He said he then would be able to read it on Saturday and call me at home Saturday night. He emphasized that he would be home all day Saturday and Saturday evening, so there was no doubt in my mind that he was serious. Further, since his Monday trip happened to be to my city, and he would be staying at a hotel near my office, he said he would call me when he arrived and set up an appointment so we could get down to specifics.

As you would expect of any good trooper, I worked several hours putting together a beautiful package that would have made Picasso proud, then hustled to beat the Federal Express cutoff at 6:00 P.M. Being an antipennywise, dollar-foolish thinker by nature, I figured the extra $10 or so for Saturday delivery was a paltry sum to pay to get the deal into high gear before Charles left town.

When I did not hear from him by Saturday evening, I thought I had better call just to make sure the package had arrived. No luck—answering machine. When I didn't hear from him by Sunday afternoon, I called again, and again got an answering machine—and, of course, no return call. Ditto Sunday evening. Because I'm sure you've been there many times yourself, you've undoubtedly already guessed that not only did I not hear from him that weekend or while he was staying at a hotel near my office on Monday and Tuesday, I never heard from him at all—as in *never again*.

**Real-World Rule No. 251: Proceed with caution when someone with whom you've had no experience enthusiastically tells you, "It sounds great. Why don't you shoot it out to me by Federal Express." If he's a Deal Gabber, the translation is, "I don't have the courage to tell you that I'm not interested, so I'll just humor you by asking you to send it Federal Express."**

While all Deal Gabbers clearly love to employ the rush-rush, send-it-by-Federal-Express routine, sometimes their need to gab is so uncontrollable that they would rather continue talking to you than pull a disappearing act. One of the most cherished ploys of a bona fide Deal Gabber is to talk endlessly about the multimillion-dollar deals he's working on—$5 million he recently invested in this deal, $10 million he invested in that deal—but when it comes to the paltry $10,000 you need for your deal, he regretfully has to pass on the opportunity. Why? Because he's "all invested up right now," or he's "having a problem that has to be cleared up first," or he's "in the middle of an expensive lawsuit." The script is always the same: "If only you had contacted me just a week earlier, I could have done the deal with no problem." Sound familiar?

People often drive themselves crazy trying to figure out why a Deal Gabber talks . . . and talks . . . and talks . . . then fails to act. But the reality is that it's not all that complicated. A Deal Gabber rarely has ill intent; he just likes to hear the sound of his own voice. He simply loves to gab. It's his mission in life, the central joy of his world of delusions. Don't waste energy getting angry at a Deal Gabber; just make it a habit never to talk business with him again.

## The Desperate Person

The Desperate Person is perhaps the most dangerous of all Drain People, because he's prone to stretching his moral beliefs. Also, a Desperate Person panics easily, making ill-advised decisions that can bring you down with him. Worst of all, because he feels he has nothing to lose, the Desperate Person is a potential lethal weapon. He can afford to try anything. When the Desperate Person reaches the frantic stage, make certain that you aren't close enough to be harmed by his bad judgment.

## The Destroyer

The Destroyer's chief objective is to tear you down, preferably by assuring you that you can't succeed at what you're trying to accomplish. If there's one thing you don't need in your life, it's someone who emphasizes negatives and tries to chip away at your confidence. Unfortunately, we live in a very negative world, and we don't have to look very far to find someone who is happy to tell us why our objectives are unattainable.

Most Destroyers are just unhappy people who continually confirm the truth of the "misery loves company" axiom. It can be like getting caught in a spider's web, because the unhappy Destroyer thrives on the opportunity to pull others down to his level. If you're not careful, such a Destroyer will soon have you prostrating yourself and relating your troubles to him. And when that happens, he will happily pontificate to you, appoint himself to become your psychiatrist, and tell you everything that's wrong with you—with a certitude that implies that *he* is problem free and totally well adjusted. His ultimate joy is to succeed in making *you* psychologically dependent upon *him*.

Another kind of Destroyer is The Expert, a narrow-minded creature who drips conventional wisdom from the corners of his permanently opened mouth. Loaded to the gills with this abundance of wisdom, he feels compelled to tear you down. The Businessworld Arena, in particular, is saturated with self-appointed experts whose chief objective seems to be to make certain that you clearly understand their superiority over you. Nurture the habit of not allowing yourself to be intimidated by experts offering conventional wisdom. In truth, conventional wisdom is nothing more than a proclamation of unknown origin stating that something can't be done, until someone too dumb to understand the proclamation comes along and does it, after which whatever he does then becomes the new conventional wisdom.

To paraphrase Viktor Frankl, an expert is nothing more than a person who no longer sees the forest of truth for the trees of facts. If you want to make The Expert—or any Destroyer, for that matter—angry, just prove him wrong. Better still, if you want to improve your chances of achieving positive results, practice the habit of eliminating him from your life.

## The Hallucinator

The Hallucinator usually is just a Desperate Person waiting to happen. His self-delusions are so extreme that they take him beyond a waking dream state into another dimension.

In the early 1980s I visited a financial newsletter writer whom I had always suspected of being a Hallucinator, though I hadn't known him well enough to be certain. He had achieved a degree of publicity for his doom-and-gloom forecasts, and, as a result, the hallucinatory cells in his brain had begun flexing their muscles. During the course of our conversation, he gazed upward and, in a matter-of-fact tone, said, "I recently had a vision that I'm going to be president of the United States."

Thinking that he was joshing me, I replied, tongue in cheek, "Great, but are you sure you want the job?"

He then looked straight at me, eyes glazed over like someone who had just returned from a ride in a spaceship, and replied, "It's already a fait accompli. The vision is clear; the wheels of history are in place. I couldn't stop it now even if I wanted to."

I was about to chuckle and one-up him with another humorous retort, but my mouth froze closed when I saw the faraway gaze in his eyes. Again, he looked upward with a blank stare, whereupon I began sizing up the distance between me and the door. "Hey," I thought to myself in horror, "this guy is serious. He really *believes* he's going to be president!" Forget the fact that he had more skeletons in his closet than Forest Lawn. His notion of reality was that he was going to be president!

The Sufi poet Jalaluddin Rumi once wrote that even Jesus fled from the fool, saying, "I can make the blind see, the deaf hear, the lame run and raise the dead, but I cannot turn the fool away from his folly." That being the case, you'd be wise to make it a habit to keep your distance from Hallucinators.

## The Liar

Remember the definition of honesty: the absolute refusal to lie, steal, cheat, or deceive in any way. I discussed this in some detail in Chapter 5, particularly as it relates to various types of lying, so we needn't look at more examples. What's important here is to emphasize that you have a right—some might argue an obligation—to hold others in your life to the same high standards to which you adhere.

Also, I can't emphasize enough how easy it is to delude yourself in this area. You must get into the habit of observing what people do, not just what they say. There is much wisdom in the proverb, Your ears are to hear only what your eyes miss. This gets back to the problem of going overboard to give people the benefit of the doubt. While that may seem like a noble gesture, it's even more noble to focus your energy on people who consistently demonstrate their honesty, people who don't *need* the benefit of the doubt. Good rule to follow: When in doubt, keep the person out—of your life.

## The Rudemonger

The Rudemonger is totally self-centered. He rarely, if ever, says *please* or *thank you;* he is continually late for meetings; he regularly interrupts telephone conversations, asking the party on the other end of the line to excuse him while he carries on a discussion with someone in his office; he is curt, insensitive, and discourteous; and, above all, he's a master at not returning phone calls and not calling people back when he says he will. Obviously, a Deal Gabber may also qualify as a Rudemonger.

The Rudemonger's usual excuse (following a profuse and flowery apology) for not returning your call is that he has been "super busy" and just hasn't had time. Because of his self-centered psyche, it doesn't occur to him that this is a double insult. First, by telling you how busy he's been, he clearly is implying that you *aren't* busy. Personally, I think people who dwell on how busy they are sound like amateurs. In the real world, I assume that *everyone* with whom I deal is busy. Second, "haven't had time" implies that you are a low priority on his list, and your chances of getting results with someone who sees you as a low priority are very slim.

Perhaps the most pragmatic reason for staunchly maintaining the habit of keeping the Rudemonger out of your life is that it's simply inefficient for you to deal with him. If you're properly focused on success, the one thing you don't have time to hear is how busy the other guy is. You should be far more concerned about how busy *you* are, because, unbeknownst to the Rude-monger, *you* probably have a lot less time for *him* than he has for you. In that light, it also becomes a matter of self-respect, because a person who doesn't value his time doesn't value himself.

## The Skinflint

The Skinflint is a first cousin to the Chiseler, but with less intelligence. Though he isn't capable of seeing it, he constantly loses out because of his obsession for acting in pennywise, dollar-foolish ways.

A few years ago, a fellow speaker called me about a book he had been working on that he was convinced would be a block-buster best-seller. (Note: To put this in proper perspective, you should understand that *every* speaker is always working on a book that he is convinced will be a blockbuster best-seller if he can just get it published.) He was aware of my experience both with publishing my own books and working with other publish-ers, and wanted to know if I would be willing to meet with him and give him some advice. Because we had a mutual friend, I agreed to do so, but told him that I would have to check my calendar and get back to him.

Before getting off the phone, he mentioned that a few years earlier he had written a self-published paperback booklet about the physical and logistical aspects of putting on seminars. During the course of my career, I, like every other writer and speaker I know of, have given away thousands of complimentary copies of my books and audio tapes, not only to friends and acquaintances, but as goodwill business gestures. Therefore, I didn't give it a second thought when I told this speaker that I really would love to receive a copy of his booklet.

As the cliché goes, there's a first time for everything. The slim little paperback arrived in the mail a few days later, *with a bill enclosed*. The bill included $9.95 for the book, plus $3.00 for postage and handling! My first instinct was to chuckle. The pennywise, dollar-foolish message was clear: "You pay me full price for my paperback booklet, including postage and handling, then give me whatever book-publishing information I need free." If this Skinflint had charged me only for his book, maybe it would have qualified as a run-of-the-mill, humorous Skinflint story. But postage and handling? We're talking legendary pennywise, dollar-foolish material here.

The Skinflint also displays a remarkable talent for feigning a grab for the dinner check, missing it, faking a cough, and turning his head away. Then, just as you reflexively move your hand toward the check, he immediately says something like, "Are you sure?" This is followed very quickly by, "Well, okay. It's very gracious of you. I'll treat next time." Sure, and Gorbachev will be starting at second base for the Reds next season. As with the Chiseler, the Skinflint can't help himself. It's a psychological disease; he's incapable of changing.

## Legalman

Finally, we get to the perpetual World Heavyweight Drain Champion, Legalman—also commonly referred to as "attorney," "lawyer," and by a variety of obscenities. Legalman is that omnipresent humanoid commonly perceived to be the answer to the majority of people's problems, both real and imagined. Given that he has a permanent hold on the top ranking, I've reserved for him a generous amount of space befitting his elevated status.

Years ago, my hobby was supporting Legalman in regal style. I flew him around the country first-class, put him up in the finest hotels, and took him to the most elegant restaurants. I used to spend endless hours with him, joking and laughing, talking sports, philosophizing, and, yes, sometimes even discussing legal matters.

One Saturday, Legalman, my accountant, and I were having a summit meeting in my office with a centimillionaire, Mr. Vulchar, regarding a deal I was trying to put together. At one point, Mr. Vulchar, who was reviewing my financial statements, looked up and said to me, "Your legal and accounting fees are higher than mine. Why in the world do you need this much legal and accounting work?"

Embarrassed, I mumbled some incoherent, inaudible excuse, after which Mr. Vulchar waved his right hand in the direction of Legalman and my accountant and bellowed, "These guys don't work for you; you work for *them*. You're a slave to these characters."

We never did put the deal together, but Mr. Vulchar's blunt observation festered inside me until I finally decided to do something about it. It took years to break my expensive addiction to Legalman, but eventually I succeeded. At the time of Mr. Vulchar's observation about my being a slave to Legalman and my accountant, my legal bills were averaging about $6,000 a month. For many years now, by contrast, my *annual* legal expenses have been virtually zero. What I finally realized is that the need to use Legalman is, for the most part, a figment of a deluded public's collective imagination.

If you implement only one piece of advice I offer in this chapter, it should be this: Make it a habit to avoid like the plague legal entanglements of any kind, especially lawsuits. Very few things in life are as disgusting and frustrating as being a party to a lawsuit and having to witness a bunch of shamelessly unprepared attorneys fake their way through years of litigation, while simultaneously doing their best to prolong it. Rarely does anyone win a lawsuit. You either lose the case and lose to your attorney (i.e., in legal fees), which means you lose big; or you win the case and *still lose to your attorney*, which in most instances means that you sustain an overall loss. Remember, your loss must be measured not only in dollars, but in time—time spent in court, answering interrogatories, meeting with Legalman, having your deposition taken, and a wide variety of other ob-scene "legal" activities.

## MASTER OF INTIMIDATION

First and foremost, Legalman is *the* master intimidator. Now, understand that I'm not referring only to the other guy's attorney. On the contrary, it's *your* attorney with whom you should be primarily concerned. Easily intimidated people simply can't comprehend that it's their own attorney from whom they most need protection. Your attorney is the one who poses the greatest threat to your solvency, and who will kill more deals for you during your lifetime than all your opponents' attorneys combined.

One of Legalman's best intimidation props is "The Certificate," which is usually prominently displayed on the wall just behind him, ideally about six inches above his head for easy client viewing. The Certificate is commonly referred to in street parlance as a law degree, and is absolutely awesome to most clients. Little wonder. After all, the government itself stands squarely behind The Certificate. That framed little piece of paper on Legalman's wall is a written confirmation that he is entitled to all the rights and privileges of the government-mandated legal monopoly in this country. And an amazing monopoly it is: Attorneys are attorneys; prosecutors are attorneys; judges are attorneys; and over half of all U.S. congressmen are attorneys. This means that Legalman *makes* the law, *argues* the law, and *interprets* the law. If ever there was a fix, this is it.

Legalman also tries to intimidate his prey by displaying an air of superior intelligence. He takes great pleasure in perpetuating this ruse through an overdose of Legalese. If you're unfamiliar with the term *Legalese*, it's a language taught in law school, the unspoken purpose of which is to thoroughly confuse clients (on both sides) and thereby put Legalman in a position to call the shots more easily. After all, how can a client argue with Legalman's logic if he has no idea what Legalman is talking about?

If Legalman didn't inundate you with an endless stream of wherefores, whereofs, and whereases, you might start to get the idea that The Certificate is just a cover for a rather easy job. This might cause you no longer to be in awe of him, which in turn might lead you to conclude that you don't need him at all. And that's something Legalman just isn't going to allow to happen if there's any way he can help it. No matter how badly he may fail in other areas, he's acutely aware that, at all costs, he must succeed in intimidating you. His very livelihood—and, just as important, his ego—depend upon it.

My own experience with Legalman has convinced me that, by and large, he not only is not particularly bright, but is incredibly lazy, too. (Why work hard if you're in on a monopoly?) This laziness tends to manifest itself as gross negligence. Legalman will be happy to talk Legalese with you all day long, but just try to get him to shut up, sit down, roll up his sleeves, and actually draft a document. Fat chance. He'll think of every excuse this side of Harvard to avoid putting pen to paper, which is why most cases are settled out of court, many on the courthouse steps the day the trial is scheduled to commence. It's a rare occasion when Legalman is prepared to go to trial. He would always rather settle than fight, providing, of course, that he's milked the case for all it's worth and has run out of stalling tactics.

## THE FINELY HONED ART

There are basically two kinds of attorneys who kill deals: those who admit it (none) and those who deny it (all).

Many of us take Legalman's deal-killing prowess for granted, but it's a finely honed art that takes years to master. It's not as easy as it was in the good old days, when all Legalman had to do was dash into the closing at the final moment and shred the deal into legal confetti without so much as working up a sweat. Today, Legalman has to be much more sophisticated and subtle about his intentions. He must pretend that he actually *wants* the deal to close. A naïve person might be inclined to ask, "Why in the world would Legalman not want a deal to close in the first place?" There are many reasons for Legalman's deal-killing antics, and all are bad from the client's viewpoint. Two of the more common ones are:

First, learned instincts. An attorney who graduated at the top of his class at Stanford Law School once told me that his legal education consisted solely of learning how to find problems. Not solve them—*find them*. In other words, Legalman usually isn't as malevolent as he may seem; it's just that deal-killing is the only thing he's been trained to do.

Second, jealousy. This ties in with Legalman's belief that he possesses innate, superior intelligence, as well as a better formal education than yours or mine. It therefore stands to reason that he has the ability to make not only better legal judgments than his clients, but better business judgments as well. Thus, Legalman uses one of his best intimidation ploys as a weapon to kill your deal. Often, he does this under the guise of renegotiating the terms of the deal, which can always be counted on as a surefire deal-killer. Shame on you if you allow this to occur, because you should never give Legalman the opportunity to be in a position to negotiate the terms of your deal in the first place, let alone *renegotiate* them.

No doubt Legalman would love to be a businessman, but in truth he doesn't have the entrepreneurial courage to come out from behind The Certificate that hangs on his wall. That's why it eats away at him so badly when he occasionally has a client who makes more money in one good closing than he makes in a whole year of client-mooching.

Loud and clear, so there's no miscommunication on this point: Don't ask Legalman for business advice! If he volunteers it (which he will, usually in subtle ways), there's no need to raise your voice. Just reach into your breast pocket, pull out your scissors (always carry scissors with you when visiting Legalman), reach across his desk, and cut off his tie exactly two and a half inches below the knot. He'll get the point. Trust me.

And remember, it's up to you to cultivate the habit of differentiating between legal and business decisions before you can be in a position to know when to muzzle Legalman.

## FEE-BUILDING TREACHERY

When it comes to fee-building, never delude yourself about Legalman's inherent conflict of interest: The quicker a deal closes or a matter is disposed of, the less he makes. It's one of those inescapable realities of life. Following are a handful of Legalman's more shameful fee-building tactics for which you must always be on the alert.

**The Chat.** This is perhaps Legalman's favorite day-to-day fee-builder. Providing you're a client who pays his bills on time, Legalman will be more than happy to chat with you by phone about anything you desire: the Super Bowl, the latest Steven Spielberg movie, how dumb some other client's attorney is, or, if there's nothing more interesting to chat about, a good old-fashioned joke will do. When it comes to fee-building, clients consistently make the mistake of falling into this trap. It's imperative to remember that talk is *not* cheap; it's expensive when talking to Legalman. **Real-World Rule No. 31: Don't call Legalman to chat. Legalman doesn't chat; he bills.**

**The Research Project.** This is another problem that stems from your being careless in your conversations with Legalman. One of his favorite tricks is to make a research project out of an innocent question on your part, which means delegating work to a legal cub. Legalman loves a good research project, even if the client doesn't specifically ask for one, because it's a great way of leveraging himself (which is a nice way of saying he can continue to evade doing any work, while making money through the efforts of an underling).

Worse, many so-called research projects turn out to be nothing more than Xeroxing scams. A number of years ago, I asked

Legalman a casual question about the legal structure of a certain type of corporation. He said he wasn't certain about the answer, but would check it out. We exchanged comments about mutual friends, travel, and other trivia for another ten or fifteen minutes, then said our good-byes. Surprise! A couple of weeks later I received a huge envelope that contained about a hundred pages copied from a variety of law books, journals, and magazines, with a cover letter explaining that one of Legalman's assistants had "researched" my question thoroughly and that he hoped the enclosed material would satisfy my inquiry. I was (naïvely) dumfounded. Even if he had sent the material free of charge, there was no way I was going to sit down and read a hundred pages of Legalese. But it *wasn't* free. A bill for $6,000 followed the package two weeks later!

It's crucial to your wallet that you develop the habit of making it clear to Legalman that you aren't interested in his performing a lot of elaborate research.

**The Meeting.** Legalman also loves to have meetings. It's easier than holding a phone receiver to his ear, he can show off the fancy offices that *you* helped pay for, and he can pontificate Legalese to his heart's content. Best of all, he doesn't have to do any drafting (i.e., work). And if the meeting involves parties from the other side of a transaction, remember that all the irrelevant chit-chat that Legalman and the other side's attorney engage in—about their upcoming Sunday golf match, for example—is going to be paid for by you.

Finally, be sure to practice the habit of challenging Legalman's bills. Legalman has an annoying habit of seeing a regular client as an annuity. Work or not, he just assumes that he has the right to bill well-paying clients each month.

### THE TRIPLE-BYPASS LEGALDECTOMY

Legalman's methodology is based on a surgical procedure developed by a legendary attorney named I. Stickitoohymn, Esq.

The operation is called a Triple-Bypass Legaldectomy, and Legalman has been in Sir Stickitoohymn's debt ever since he first developed this operation centuries ago. If you've never undergone this delicate surgical procedure, I can best describe it as the pain you might expect to experience if you were to submit to simultaneous root-canal work and a hemorrhoid operation.

In a Triple-Bypass Legaldectomy, Legalman (1) intimidates his client, (2) kills his client's deal, and (3) removes a malignant growth of money from his client's bank account. In really extreme cases, Legalman may manage to remove *all* money from his client's bank account—malignant, benign, or otherwise. If you find it unavoidable to engage the services of Legalman, be sure to check your cash reserves. You're going to need them if his prognosis calls for a Triple-Bypass Legaldectomy.

In wrapping up Legalman (interesting choice of words), I want to make it absolutely clear that nothing I've said here should be taken as a blanket generalization. On the contrary, even though former Chief Justice Warren E. Burger stated that he believes lawyers generally overcharge their clients, and that law schools and bar associations neglect professional ethics, an innate sense of fairness compels me to point out that it's really only about 97 percent of the attorneys in this country who are lazy, incompetent, negligent, and greedy—yet they make a bad name for the entire profession! In fact, some of my best friends are . . . well, on second thought, strike that. Just concentrate on nurturing the habit of keeping Legalman out of your life to the greatest extent possible.

## Just Doing What They're Supposed to Do

The list of Drain People goes on and on: the Complainer, the Finger Pointer, the Guiltmonger, the Irrational, the Sadist, the Self-Righteous, the Silver Tongue, the Territorial Person, the Thin Skin, and many, many more. What all Drain People have in common is that they drain you of time, energy, peace of mind, relaxation, comfort, and/or money.

Interpersonal conflicts waste time and energy, and Drain People are masters at causing interpersonal conflicts. The bottom line is that Drain People are a drain. If you allow Drain People to remain in your life, your mind will be cluttered with negative emotions. This hinders your ability to concentrate on worthy people, individuals who have the potential to add value to your life, and you to theirs.

Finally, don't drive yourself crazy trying to figure out why a Drain Person acts the way he does. To paraphrase Jim Rohn, liars are supposed to lie; cheaters are supposed to cheat; complainers are supposed to complain. Unless you've decided to open a Drain People Rehabilitation Center, or you're a psychiatrist getting paid for your analyses, forget the *why*. Once and for all: Drain People are *supposed* to drain. It's their life's work. Don't question it; just concentrate on religiously practicing the Drain People Elimination Habit. It's a habit about which you have to be ever vigilant, because if you become lax you run the danger of allowing that one Drain Person into your life who could cause you a major, irreversible problem that could shatter everything you've worked to achieve.

# Chapter 9

# The Self-Discipline Habit

"Be first the master of yourself, and only then a master of others," advised Baltasar Gracián. Mastering yourself is not the easiest of tasks, because within each of us exists a perpetual struggle between our intellect and our emotions. And that's what self-discipline is all about: acting on your intellectual conclusions and overriding your instinctive desire for instant gratification. A truly self-disciplined individual is able to do this even when his emotions are running high.

Self-discipline manifests itself as a feeling of self-control. Contrary to the pop-psych preachings of our modern era, freedom does not come from "letting it all hang out" or taking a devil-may-care attitude. Freedom comes from triumphing over your emotions and proving to yourself that you can be master of your destiny. When you allow your emotions to rule, you subject yourself to emotional enslavement, and never is a person less free than when he is enslaved by his emotions.

My discussion of the Present Living Habit in Chapter 4 was not intended to imply that you should totally ignore the future. My emphasis was on striving *toward* future goals by working at something that adds meaning to your life. However, living in the present does not mean that you should take any action that happens to make you feel good today without regard to tomorrow's consequences.

Understanding that our emotions tend to be oriented toward immediate gratification is an essential first step toward developing the Self-Discipline Habit. Unfortunately, the Natural Law of Balance assures us that those things that provide the greatest amount of immediate pleasure usually are the very things most detrimental to our long-term health, happiness, and success. It's important to distinguish between the immediate, day-to-day enjoyment to be found in doing one's work—in having a meaningful life—and trying to enjoy the fruits of one's work before they have been earned.

## Future-Oriented Thinking

What I'm talking about here is future-oriented thinking—connecting today's actions with tomorrow's results. No matter how much you enjoy living in the present, prudence dictates that you take the future into consideration. Don't make the mistake of thinking of the long term as some vague point in time that will never make its appearance. It will, and almost always sooner than you anticipate. As I pointed out in Chapter 4, the future has an annoying habit of arriving ahead of schedule.

Again, it's a matter of developing a correct perception of reality, and, as discussed earlier, that's something that requires knowledge and wisdom. So long as you have a reasonable store of knowledge and wisdom, the one excuse for doing the wrong thing that is never valid is, "I didn't have a choice; I *had* to do it."

This "nonexcuse excuse" is used repeatedly by people who continually fail. They refuse to admit to themselves that it is within their power *not* to do the wrong thing if their intellect tells them that the long-term consequences are likely to be destructive. The alternative is to pay the short-term price of immediate discomfort in exchange for enjoying greater rewards over the long term. It's worth repeating: You *always* have a choice. For example, an individual who has not developed the Self-Discipline Habit may repeatedly yield to the temptation to do business with someone who has caused him problems in the past. The consequences of such a mistake are often great enough to have a major bearing on an individual's success or failure over the long term.

The person who succeeds and the person who fails at the same endeavor may both know *how* to succeed, but often there is one major difference between them: The successful person disciplines himself to *do* the right thing, whereas the unsuccessful individual allows his emotions to prevail. Charles DeGaulle admitted to his weakness in this area when he said, "I'm often wrong in what I do, but rarely wrong in what I predict."

As with all habits, self-discipline is a learned art, and to master this art requires two basic steps: First, you must consistently analyze the probable, long-term consequences of your actions. Second, you must be tenacious in *acting* in accordance with what you have determined to be in your long-term best interests.

## Cracked Mousse

A good example of implementing these two steps is reflected in an experience I had in 1984. The producer of "ABC News Nightline" called me and said he would like to do a show on "fear in the workplace." He had lined up Harold Geneen, former chairman of ITT, and a psychiatrist from Wharton to be two of the guests. He said that because my name was synonymous with intimidation, he felt I would be the ideal third guest. Shades of the old days! I told him that even though I admired Ted Koppel and thought it would be interesting to do the show, my being on the show probably would be unfair to him. I explained that *Winning Through Intimidation* had been badly miscast by the media, emphasizing that it was not a book about how to get ahead by intimidating others. The producer claimed he understood, and again urged me to do the show. Finally, I agreed to do it, but warned him that I had given up playing the intimidation clown years ago and that Koppel might be less than thrilled with my answers. Again the producer assured me that he fully understood, and the deal was on.

Notwithstanding the producer's assurances, however, Koppel's opening question to me was, "Mr. Ringer, you've been called 'the Apostle of Intimidation.' How do you feel about motivating workers through fear?"

Sound the trumpets, the moment had arrived. I had taken the trouble to analyze the long-term consequences of my actions before coming to the studio, and I was determined to follow through and act in what I had concluded were my long-term best interests. I fully recognized that it *was* within my power to demonstrate self-discipline and say what I really felt, rather than go along with the producer's hoped-for, three-ring circus as I had done so many times earlier in my career. In a serious, calm tone, I said to Koppel, "Well, Ted, first of all I have to take exception to the label 'Apostle of Intimidation.' " Koppel twitched, his hair mousse cracked, and the interview went downhill from there. As you might have guessed, the program was a dud. Though I felt bad for the producer, I had warned him that I would not go along with playing the bad guy in an extemporaneous intimidation skit, and he had assured me that the show was not going to go in that direction.

The moral is that just because you've failed to exercise good sense and self-discipline in the past (as I had with *Time* magazine and the rest of the media earlier in my career) doesn't mean that you have to continue to do so. Remember: It *always* is within your power to act in your long-term best interests.

## Conquering the Impulsive Urge

People generally fall into one of two groups when it comes to the basis of their actions. Individuals tend to act either on impulse or on self-discipline, and it's pretty obvious which type of individual tends to succeed and which type tends to fail. Acting

impulsively—in knee-jerk-response fashion—to what is going
on around you equates to an out-of-control and dangerous life.
Nonetheless, we are continually tempted to act impulsively,
and impulsive action is based on emotion rather than intellect or
common sense.

## Immunity Not Granted

In the marketplace, as untold millions have discovered, the
consequences of acting impulsively by joining the actions of the
crowd can be catastrophic. The so-called lemming effect (one
person following another over the edge of a financial cliff) has
fascinated students of human nature for centuries. The condition of your Self-Discipline Habit is severely tested when the
crowd is heading in one direction and your intellect and/or common sense tells you that it's the *wrong* direction. That's when
you must exercise the self-discipline to override the momentary
comfort of being in the mainstream. When you're tempted to
act impulsively in a situation such as this, remind yourself that
the mainstream doesn't do very well over the long term. Civilization progresses as a result of the actions of a few great minds;
the mainstream then simply goes along for the ride—and usually too late, at that.

The real estate wizard I mentioned in Chapter 1 certainly was
not alone in his overzealousness toward real estate. He just
happened to be a highly visible victim of the madness-of-the-
real-estate-crowd syndrome. The worst epidemic of the so-
called boom mentality in real estate in the 1980s took place just
south of the U.S. border in a large, unruly nation known as
*Texas*. In the late 1970s and early 1980s, I often commented to
acquaintances in Texas that perhaps they should scale back
their building activities since the rest of the country was coming
apart at the seams.

But scaling back was unthinkable. The only question was
whether Texas real estate developers would laugh or get mad at
you for daring to speak in such a preposterous fashion. The

typical response was something to the effect of, "Oh, recession doesn't happen in Texas. We're pretty much immune. It's a whole different ball game here." And, as they say, the rest is history. The bankruptcy courts in this "immune" area of North America are still trying to catch up with the last-minute rush. If you're not a famous heart surgeon, a former Secretary of the Treasury, or a once-skyrocketing billionaire, you don't even rate a second glance on the Texas bankruptcy court dockets.

As always, when the real estate boom in Texas heats up again—and you can be sure it will—those who have the self-discipline to get out long before the next bubble bursts will be the ones who come out ahead.

## A Dangerous Arena for Impulsive Souls

An individual is particularly susceptible to impulsive action in the heat of negotiating situations. If a person becomes involved in high-level negotiations without first having cultivated the Self-Discipline Habit, he's likely to end up looking like he had a run-in with The Terminator. I know, because I have the scars to prove it.

### Beware "Too Good to Be True"

You have to be careful not to give a knee-jerk *yes* when someone makes a satisfactory counteroffer, or, worse, a counteroffer that seems too good to be true. Almost without fail, the instinct that tells you that something sounds too good to be true turns out to be correct. Unfortunately, if you make the mistake of being too fast on the *yes*, the realities usually don't dawn on you until hours after the meeting ends. You're driving on the freeway, smiling contently, and all at once it hits you—the key point you failed to take into consideration when you impulsively agreed to that too-good-to-be-true counteroffer! You suddenly realize that you either have to take a financial bloodbath or compromise your moral standards by backing out of a deal to which you have already agreed.

The best defense against making this kind of mistake is to set a firm policy that you won't agree to any offer—no matter how good it may sound—before calling time-out and carefully analyzing it in private. Preferably, you should think about it at least overnight. If you can't get that much time, try to get a few hours. And if that's not feasible, ask for fifteen minutes. Anything is better than a knee-jerk *yes,* so the important thing is to maintain the self-discipline to ask for as much time as you can get.

## A CLEVER THING TO SAY

Good listening not only promotes good human relations, it's also pragmatic. Will Durant, after spending seventy years researching and writing about world civilizations, concluded, "Nothing is often a good thing to do, and almost always a clever thing to say."

Heeding Durant's advice, I've tried hard over the years to repress my impulse to jump in and talk at the first sign of an opening. Particularly when negotiating, I've disciplined myself to let the other guy talk . . . and talk . . . and talk . . . while I listen . . . listen . . . listen. I recall being on the other side of the table in a negotiating situation when the other party made the mistake of talking when he should have been listening. During a final negotiating session, I started to list the terms I would accept, and after stating that I wanted A, B, and C, he suddenly interrupted me and said, "I know, I know—and you want D, E, and F." To my surprise, he had rattled off what he thought were the figures I was about to state. However, the figures he stated were much *higher* than those I had in mind. Trying to mask my excitement, I quickly said, "Right! Right! We're completely in tune. How did you ever guess? That's exactly what I was going to say!"

Sure enough, those were the precise terms upon which we closed the deal. The other party's little error—not having the self-discipline to hear me out before talking—ended up costing him an additional $180,000. That's about $16,000 a word! A very high price to pay for not developing the habit of controlling the urge to talk.

## TRUMP CARDS AND GREED

Here's one for graduate students only: Nurture the self-discipline to head off the impulse to cavalierly throw out trump cards when negotiating. The purpose of trump cards is to trump, so always hold back a couple of cards for the finale. Almost without fail, you'll need to call on one or more of them as the going gets tough in the closing stages. The wise negotiator always keeps something in reserve, because experience has taught him that there's no such thing as a smooth closing. He knows that he's going to need a trump card or two when the inevitable renegotiation process begins. Again, that's *re*negotiation.

Also, if you're careless about using your trump cards, you open yourself to the Human Greed Factor, which works like this: If you suggest the possibility of doing X, providing the other party will go along with Y, often the other party will reject Y, but insist that X be part of the deal. Dirty pool, true; nonetheless, sharp negotiators have been using this cute little tactic since the time Cro-Magnon man first appeared on earth. All other things being equal, you're better off to save X as a trump card to be used near the finish line when a concession is needed to get the deal closed. **Real-World Rule No. 168: Any time you introduce a compromise chip into a negotiation, it has a mysterious way of becoming a firm part of the deal in the other party's mind.**

Also, recognize that one of the best ways to hoard trump cards is to yield on as many nonessential points as possible. It's a matter of controlling the impulse to reject a point just because you feel it's inequitable. The results-oriented question is not whether or not something is equitable; the more important question is, how much does it really matter? In fact, you should be *anxious* to yield on as many nonessential points as possible, because the more times you give in, the easier it is to get the other side to concede on those points that *are* essential to you. In the heat of negotiations, don't allow false pride to interfere when it comes to yielding on nonessential points. Remember, self-discipline is a matter of intellect overruling emotion. Your focus should not be on winning as many points as possible; it should be on gaining your *main objective*.

## THE DEAL-KILLING BONUS

A dealmaker, or negotiator, is really just a good salesman, so he should try to heed all the prudent rules that apply to good salesmanship. And every good salesman knows the danger of kicking an open door; i.e., continuing to sell after the prospect has already agreed to buy. The smart salesman or negotiator knows when to stop selling and negotiating, and develops the self-discipline to act accordingly. The more you talk, the more you increase your chances of saying something that may open a can of worms and kill a deal at the eleventh hour. In particular, never get carried away and introduce into a deal one or more after-the-fact bonuses in the form of new ideas, people, or thoughts. This can prove to be a very costly mistake, one that often results in reopening negotiations—or, worse, killing a deal that was already in the bag.

Such impulsive action calls to mind a deal I had been negotiating for a couple of months back in the early 1970s. It involved an investor in Philadelphia regarding a distributorship for a high-quality line of health-care products. I had already made two trips to Philadelphia to discuss the deal with him, and we had spoken by phone about a dozen times. During each meeting and telephone discussion, we edged closer and closer to agreeing on a deal. Finally, after my second trip to Philadelphia, we ironed out the final details and shook hands on a verbal agreement, after which I flew back to the West Coast.

We then spoke again by phone and set up a closing date in Philadelphia. Having been involved in more than one deal in the past where the other party failed to do what he said he was going to do, I took the trouble, during our telephone discussion, to review carefully each point we had agreed upon. I wanted to be absolutely certain that there was no miscommunication between us before I made the long trip back to Philadelphia. The investor was the impatient type, and several times during my review he interrupted me with comments like, "Hey, relax, it's a 'done deal.' " I guess it's something in my genetic makeup, but the more times he repeated the words *done deal*, the more uncomfortable I became.

Politely brushing aside his assurances, I persisted in my review of the points. The last item I brought up was something called *money*. It hadn't gone unnoticed by me over the years that the words *write out a check* seem to do funny things to people—like make them frown, or quiver, or don their Darth Vader personality—or do something more subtle, like threaten you with a hunting knife. So I clearly and slowly said, "And then, *you'll write me a check for $200,000.*"

The investor impatiently replied, "Yes, yes. I said we've got a deal. Just fly to Philadelphia and let's get this thing closed."

And that's when I did something that forever qualified me for the **All-World Entrepreneurial Dumb Team.** Even though we supposedly had a deal, my insecurity led me to throw in an afterthought bonus just to make sure. Displaying an alarming lack of self-discipline, I blurted out, "I have a great idea. Why don't I invite a couple of the top marketing people from this company to come to Philadelphia and meet with us? Then we can talk about the company's future plans just before or after the closing, and kill two birds with one stone." The investor liked my idea and told me to go ahead and set everything up.

After arriving in Philadelphia, the investor and I met with Legalman and reviewed the final details of the closing. Then, after finishing our review, Legalman went to his office to dictate the final changes to his secretary, assuring us that the papers would be ready for signing in an hour or so. To pass the time, the investor and I made small talk, waiting until either Legalman brought in the closing documents or the marketing people showed up. For the sake of making conversation, I again casually started to review some of the points of the deal, and again the investor interrupted me, chuckled, and said, "Boy, you really are the nervous type. It's a done deal, forget it. Let's just concentrate on the game plan for marketing these products."

Just about that time, the marketing people arrived, and we decided to meet with them right away since the final draft of the agreement was not yet completed. Unless you, too, are a member of the **All-World Entrepreneurial Dumb Team,** you wouldn't believe what took place at that meeting. For a battle-scarred entrepreneur like me, it was like living through *The Chainsaw Massacre.* Every time one of the marketing executives spoke, the investor would say something like, "Hmm, I didn't know that. Why is that so?" Or, "You mean you can't really be sure of that? Then it might require more money than we'll have available?" And worse . . . and worse . . . and worse.

I, of course, took it very well, crying out loud only twice and using up only one box of Kleenex. After the meeting, the investor and I went to what was supposed to have been the closing room and waited for Legalman to bring in the closing documents. But there was an inexplicable feeling in the air that made me uncomfortable, so I casually started to review some of the closing points yet again. As quickly as possible I got to the words that must be spoken, sooner or later, at every closing— what I like to refer to as the "getting paid" words—virtually the same words I had uttered to the investor by phone before committing to come to Philadelphia: "And *then*, you'll give *me* the check for $200,000—"

Whereupon the investor interrupted me with—you guessed it—"What check?"

And people wonder why our mental institutions are overflowing with psychotic entrepreneurs foaming at the mouth?

The investor then went into a long dissertation, saying that he apologized profusely if there had been a "miscommunica-tion," but that he had had no idea that I was coming in from the West Coast with the intention of closing a deal. He insisted that he had been under the impression that the purpose of our meet-ing was to talk to the marketing people, after which we would see if we could "agree on a marketing plan" (whatever that was supposed to mean). Then, so went his story, we were supposed to decide whether or not we could work out a deal, and, if so, set a date for a closing.

Quite an interesting miscommunication, given the fact that nothing remotely close to any of this had ever been discussed by either of us previously, and the marketing people were there only as a result of a stupid afterthought on my part. Further, not one word about any of this had been mentioned when the in-vestor, Legalman, and I had reviewed the final closing points just prior to the marketing people showing up, nor when Le-galman had said that he was going to dictate the final corrections for the closing documents.

I had to confess to myself that, through an inexcusable lack of self-discipline, it was I alone who had been responsible for reopening a done deal. It was I who had thoughtlessly and impulsively introduced new people into the deal before it was officially closed . . . and, as a result, I ended up taking a rick-shaw back to the West Coast.

## LIFETIME MEMBERSHIP

Since I seem to be on a dumb roll here, I might as well let you hear The Big Dumb—how I one-upped myself, outdoing even my Philadelphia caper. This is the one that put me on the *All-Time,* **All-World Entrepreneurial Dumb Team,** the clas-sic act-on-impulse-and-live-to-regret-it mistake.

Long before I had written my first book, I was involved in a corporation with a very wealthy partner who had a tidy little financial statement of about $13 million (a figure closer to $30 million in today's dollars). After a long series of negotiations, our corporation agreed to buy a printing plant for a substantial amount of cash and a promissory note of approximately $500,000. Everything was a go, except that the owners of the printing plant wanted my wealthy partner personally to guarantee the note. He finally agreed to do so, and at that point the deal was seemingly done.

However, at the closing one of the two sellers blurted out, sort of as an afterthought, "Why don't you (yes, *me!*) guarantee the note, too?" To which I chuckled in return, "If Frank can't pay the $500,000, it sure isn't going to do you any good to have me on the note. He's worth $13 million; I'm worth $11.83 (which was an exaggeration, since I had forgotten to deduct the $5.50 service charge from my last bank statement). The seller, with an I-may-as-well-give-it-one-more-shot attitude, retorted, "Heck, if that's true, then what's the difference? If you're not worth anything, and Frank has the big financial statement, what have you got to lose? It just shows some added good faith on your part."

The seller was not noted for having oversized brain cells, so I think he just got lucky. In point of fact, however, he had said exactly what someone in his position *should* say. Anytime you have everything to gain and nothing to lose, *try it*. One never knows what strange turns life may take down the road. On the other hand, my severe case of impulsitis was not yet in remission, so I said exactly what someone in my position should *not* say: "Okay, no big deal. It's meaningless, but I'll do it."

Years later, life had taken the following strange turns:

1. The company with which I was no longer associated was not able to pay the note.

2. My ex-partner, after a record-setting string of masochistic financial decisions, filed for bankruptcy.

3. And guess who became a highly visible, best-selling author with a considerably higher bank balance than $11.83? A

bank balance, I should add, that soon was reduced by an amount of about $500,000.

To this day, I'm certain that had I held my ground and refused to guarantee the note, the seller would have shrugged it off and the deal still would have closed. It was an expensive way to learn that when the urge to say *yes* comes over you in situations in which the down side has the potential to be pretty nasty, that's precisely when you need the self-discipline to say *no*. As I found out, an impulsive *yes* can have devastating consequences for years to come. In the most extreme cases, it can ruin an entire lifetime.

## The Lazy Man's Way to Disaster

One of the most costly results of an individual's failure to embrace the Self-Discipline Habit is that he continually falls victim to the dreaded Assumption Trap. The words *I assumed* comprise one of the most dangerous phrases in the English language. Everyone past the Age of Infinite Wisdom is all too aware that it's unwise to assume anything, yet most people stumble through life over a road laced with land-mine assumptions.

An important step toward avoiding the Assumption Trap is to learn to translate Assumptionese. For example, "I assume" usually means "I'm just too lazy to check out the facts." "No problem" in Assumptionese means "I told someone else to take care of it, so it's not *my* problem." And so it goes. Most people will expend incredible amounts of energy to avoid expending the energy needed to do the job they were asked to do in the first place.

It's an absolutely amazing phenomenon, but there seems to be a totally unwarranted, broadly accepted assumption on the part of the public that someone, somewhere, is in control of everything. However, the longer I live, the more convinced I am that *no one* is in control of *anything*. The fact is that we're living on a runaway planet! There's only one safe assumption in life: The person who assures you that everything is all right is all wrong.

## Being There

I've given the Assumption Trap a lot of thought since I saw an intriguing movie several years ago. The movie *Being There*, starring the late Peter Sellers, is about a functionally illiterate gardener who had never been outside of his own yard until well into middle age. Suddenly, through a series of bizarre happenstances, he is brought into Washington's inner circles and hailed as a brilliant statesman.

Because the illiterate gardener has had almost no experience in communicating, when he is asked his name, he mutters his occupation instead: *gardener*. As a result, the political power brokers mistakenly conclude that his name is Chauncey Gardener. He is interviewed on television, invited to the White House to meet the president, and introduced to the city's elite at a series of gala affairs. As the movie concludes, political insiders are considering the possibility of having Chauncey run for president because of his "impeccable qualifications."

While it would appear that *Being There* is nothing more than a farfetched comedy about incompetence rising to the top, I have my own theory about the film's success. Deep down within the recesses of even the most ignorant and naïve moviegoer's brain is the uncomfortable feeling that *Being There* depicts real life! Consider:

—I once had a business relationship with a well-known "psychotherapist" who, to this day, frequently appears on national television (introduced as a psychologist) and offers advice to millions of viewers, yet doesn't even have a degree in psychology! Further, I've been present on numerous occasions when this "psychologist" has, behind closed doors, screamed and yelled hysterically, cried uncontrollably, or both. Off camera, he uses foul language in virtually every sentence, and admits to never reading newspapers, magazines, or books. Early on I was surprised to find that it was difficult for a reasonably well-informed person even to discuss psychology with him, because he simply hadn't read much about the subject! Nevertheless, this Being There individual is still billed on television as an expert psychologist, and millions of people assume that he is eminently qualified. After all, if he weren't, why would he be on television?

—Another Being There example that comes to mind was passed along to me by a brilliant heart specialist who once told me that a certain nationally renowned heart surgeon was a bona fide joke among his peers at the university where he taught. While he was being given national attention for his supposedly miraculous achievements in heart surgery, the consensus among his peers was that he shouldn't be performing surgery *at all* because of his lack of surgical skills!

I'm sure you could cite similar Being There examples from your own experience. The question is, how do such people manage to get into positions of wealth, fame, and/or power? How are they able to delude the public into believing they are something other than what they really are? In many cases, it's because we generally assume that what we hear on television and read in newspapers represents truth. Unfortunately, a large percentage of the time nothing could be further from the truth. You have to exercise the self-discipline to work at seeing what *is* rather than what *seems* to be. Buddha gave us sound advice in this area, too, when he said, "Believe nothing, no matter where you read it, or who said it, no matter if I have said it, unless it agrees with your own reason and your own common sense."

## The Long Way to Toronto

One of the most time-wasting experiences of my life occurred in the early 1970s, and was a direct result of my falling into the Assumption Trap. In Chapter 5, I mentioned that a business associate and I had purchased a controlling interest in an American Stock Exchange company. My associate, John, was perhaps the most action-oriented individual I have ever known, but, as is so often the case with action types, he was totally unconcerned with details. His complete disregard for facts and planning often created an amazing entanglement of problems, and situations so bizarre they could have passed for slapstick comedy skits.

To close the deal, we needed to borrow $1.8 million. John had a long-standing relationship with the chief operating officer of a bank in London, going back to the days when the banker (who was an American) had lived in the United States. However, John had not dealt with this banker since he had moved to England. John told me that if I went to London to talk to the banker about the loan, he would call ahead of time and "set everything up."

I was delighted to have the opportunity to walk into a roll-out-the-carpet situation, and as soon as John spoke with his banker friend, I booked my flight to London. It was an exhausting, all-night trip, and when I arrived in London about 9:00 A.M. I hopped in a cab and went directly to the bank. I introduced myself to the receptionist, and was soon led into the banker's office. Though I was exhausted, I was totally focused on the $1.8 million loan I hoped to obtain. The banker and I exchanged pleasantries, after which he got right to the point and asked, "Well, Mr. Ringer, what can I do for you?" I explained that my partner and I wanted to borrow $1.8 million to buy control of an American Stock Exchange company, whereupon he interrupted me and said, "Oh, I'm afraid you've come to the wrong branch. That would be considered a venture-capital loan, and we only make conventional loans here. You'll have to see the people at our Toronto branch."

As I walked out the front door of the bank, I thought to myself, "I must make it a point to fly to London more often. What a perfectly delightful experience." There's nothing quite as exhilarating as flying across the ocean, staggering half asleep to a bank, meeting with the chief loan officer for five minutes, then being told that you've come to the wrong branch and that the branch you want is an hour's flying time from where you started. But at least I was assured of a continuing spot on the **All-Time, All-World Entrepreneurial Dumb Team.**

When I reached Heathrow Airport, I called John in the States and put on an Oscar-winning performance of pretending as though it was no big deal. "John," I queried, "I thought you said you had already discussed this matter with your banker? He had no idea what I had come to talk to him about, and right off the bat told me that I'd have to talk to the bank's Toronto branch about this kind of loan."

"Well, of course I didn't go into detail with him over the phone," snapped John. "I just told him I would appreciate if it he would meet with an associate of mine about a deal we were working on together. No sense trying to explain the deal long-distance."

I stopped chewing the phone cord just long enough to smile and say, "My fault, John. I just assumed you had already explained the deal to him. What do you suggest now?"

Without a pause, John said, "Look, I'll call the Toronto branch and explain the whole thing to them, then you can fly straight to Toronto. Call me back in a half hour."

Sure enough when I called back, he had spoken to the Toronto branch and set up another appointment for—would you believe?—later that day. "No problem," I assured him, "I'll be there." I wrote down all the pertinent information—names, telephone numbers, and addresses—and, after bidding John farewell, called the bank's branch in Toronto and asked to speak to the officer with whom I was to meet. I not only reconfirmed our appointment, but also explained the deal to him in detail. *I assumed nothing.* Then, *after* he had assured me that his bank would be interested, I departed for Toronto.

Luckily, the story had a happy ending, because the loan eventually was granted. However, unless you want to end up in bizarre situations like flying to England for a five-minute rejection, don't assume that someone else has checked the facts. If it's your body that's going to take the punishment, it's up to you to have the self-discipline to do the checking before swinging into action. The bigger the stakes, the truer it is, especially when you approach paydirt. **Real-World Rule No. 357: At the moment of truth, never risk a fumble. When the ball is on the one-yard line, carry it over yourself.**

## The Reality of Miscommunications

Speaking of costly assumptions, it's also important to remember **Real-World Rule No. 244: The degree of miscommunication regarding what's been agreed upon in a business deal tends to increase in direct proportion to the amount of money involved.**

Never assume that all parties to an important meeting have the same understanding of what's been agreed upon. I make it a practice to take copious notes at all such meetings, then have the notes copied and see to it that everyone present reviews them before leaving. I also read the notes aloud, then ask if anyone has any questions. If someone misunderstands, or disagrees, with one of the points, we talk it out, make the appropriate corrections, again have the notes copied, and repeat the same process until everyone agrees on what has been agreed upon.

Does this totally eliminate misunderstandings? No, of course not. Life isn't that simple. However, if one of the parties decides he wants to change, or back out of, the deal, it does make it much more difficult for him to use the phony excuse that "apparently there was a miscommunication between us."

## My Encounter with Ms. Best

Interviewing prospective employees is another area in which I've learned the hard way to adhere to the Self-Discipline Habit when it comes to making assumptions. In an age when young people believe they should be rewarded just for being alive, a large percentage of job applicants have a remarkably inflated perception of their abilities. Many applicants today can't even spell the word *competency* let alone display it in their work. Therefore, it's a dangerous mistake to assume that just because someone talks confidently in an interview, he is what he appears to be. There's many a slip between the interview and a person's performance on the job.

My own frustrating experience in this area has taught me to be especially wary when an individual makes too forceful a case for himself. It seems as though a whole cult of people has grown up who, lacking skill, competence, and/or ambition, have become amazingly adept at fooling interviewers. The objective today isn't to become competent at a job; it's to become competent at being interviewed. Early in my career, I thought I was quite good at judging prospects during interviews, but, without being consciously aware of it, I apparently lost pace with the rapid proliferation of interviewee tricks.

My memory takes me back to a frantic search for a high-level "executive secretary." (I use quote marks around the words *executive secretary* because it seems as though anyone who knows how to type fifty words a minute, talks in an authoritative tone on the telephone, and has managed to stay with one employer for at least six months fancies himself an executive secretary.) After I'd interviewed a number of prospects, one candidate in particular made a big impression on me with her air of self-confidence. In fact, at one point she just came right out and told me, in a matter-of-fact tone, that she was "the best." Of course, because she was the best she also wanted a starting salary that was far in excess of anything I had previously paid to unproven talent. You're probably thinking, "Well, knowing Ringer, he took the bait." And you're right.

Naïvely, I assumed that this young lady must, at the very least, be very good. Otherwise, how would she have the nerve to come right out and say she was *the best?* To make such a bold statement, she must have *something* to back it up with, I reasoned. Since I was not able to contact her previous employer (naturally, he was out of business, apparently living in Sri Lanka or somewhere, and unavailable for comment), I based the hiring of her on my assumptions.

After a couple of weeks, I noticed a few things that Ms. Best was doing wrong, but I wasn't too concerned about them because I had the comfort of knowing that she was "the best." After all, she had told me so. While tactfully complimenting her on her "progress," I also casually suggested that there were a few areas where she might want to sharpen up a bit—such as trying not to make so many assumptions herself (which seemed to be leading her to make numerous mistakes), being more alert when listening to dictation (so as to make fewer of *those* mistakes), and cutting down on her social calls during business hours (always a mistake).

By the third month, I was ready to concede that Ms. Best was not "the best" after all. To those in the office who were thinking more in terms of setting the back of her hair on fire, I said, "Look, maybe she isn't the superstar I thought she was, but she is good. She just seems to have mental lapses now and then."

By the end of the fourth month, I was beginning to weaken. "All right, I admit she makes a lot of mistakes. I admit she sometimes forgets to write down phone messages. I admit she has a habit of making costly assumptions. But she *is* mechanically proficient," I protested in desperation.

By the fifth month, it was *I* who was considering putting a torch to her hair. I finally threw in the towel one day when I called Ms. Best into my office to point out another mistake she had made, one that had resulted in some costly repercussions. My primary intent was to forestall a repetition of the unhappy event, but she didn't let it go at that. Her first reaction was to tell me that it was *I* who was mistaken, that my recollection of my own instructions was incorrect. After I strongly suggested that my instructions had been as I had stated, Ms. Best broke into tears and ran out of my office. It certainly was a touching sight—extraordinarily appropriate business behavior for an "executive secretary."

Subsequently, she reviewed her transcription notes and found, to her chagrin, that she had been wrong. Did that prompt her to offer a brief and immediate apology? Of course not, that's not the way "the best" operate. Instead, she typed up a two-page explanation of the situation—on company time—in which she admitted her mistake, but emphasized that "[my] handling of the situation begged for defensive action on [her] part."

At that point, I realized that I had an important decision to make: Either I had to go into the professional baby-sitting business full-time or admit to the rest of the office that I had been guilty of making an embarrassing and incorrect assumption. I decided on the latter. Not only was Ms. Best guilty of all the aforementioned goof-ups, but, my previous assertions notwithstanding, she really was not even mechanically proficient.

Alas, the truth had to be acknowledged. If Ms. Best was "the best," I was the Dalai Lama of Tibet. She was *not* the best; she was *not* good; she was *not* average; she was *not even bad*. She was, in point of fact, the *worst* secretary I had ever hired—a living, breathing, full-fledged incompetent, fit only for employment by a government agency.

Job applicants with inflated self-perceptions are primarily guilty of self-delusion; i.e., they base their actions on who and what they would like to be rather than who and what they really are. Get into the habit of not assuming that someone is even marginally competent, no matter how good he claims to be. Instead, have the self-discipline to make him *prove* it through performance. And if he's not willing to prove it, have the self-discipline to pass.

## Winning by Default

David Seabury succinctly expressed a great deal of wisdom when he stated, "The hero is not impulsive. He prepares." One of the best aids to bolster your self-discipline is to make it a point to be prepared.

Basically, preparation involves two areas. First is factual and/or tangible preparation, which includes figures, documents, and various materials that can aid you in stating your case in a favorable manner. Second is psychological preparation, the ultimate of which is to mentally rehearse a variety of likely scenarios in advance. By anticipating an objection before a meeting takes place, you're in a position to head it off in the event someone brings it up. Better still, you yourself can raise the question of a potential obstacle before the other side even thinks of it, phrasing it in such a way that it appears to be an item that can be handled with ease.

Since I've just related a couple of zingers about myself, this may seem hard to believe, but one of my greatest strengths is having the self-discipline to prepare. My numerous past indiscretions in this area have caused me to become fanatically disciplined when it comes to preparation. "If I had eight hours to chop down a tree, I'd spend six sharpening my axe," said Abraham Lincoln. I'd like to tell you that Abe stole that line from me, but you'd never buy it. Nonetheless, I normally practice this philosophy when I undertake a project. I like to lay the groundwork slowly and carefully, then, when all is in place, sprint to the finish line. Before I meet with someone to make a presentation or discuss a business proposal, I make certain that I do my homework. It's wise to go into a meeting armed with the facts. In the words of Pythagoras, "Numbers have a way of taking a man by the hand and leading him down the path of reason."

Since most people rarely are well prepared, I look at it almost like winning by default. If you and I are otherwise even in all pertinent aspects of a deal, you lose. Why? Because unless I fall into one of my rare laziness lapses, I will outprepare you. My objective, quite frankly, is to literally overwhelm you with preparation. I'm not one of those people who enjoys close games; I like victories that are as one-sided as a plane crash.

This isn't arrogance on my part. On the contrary, I freely admit that it takes no innate skill or intelligence. I *learned* to do it, because I observed, through firsthand experience, that it leads to big payoffs. And the more big payoffs I achieved, the more motivated I became to be prepared. On reflection, many of my greatest successes have been a result of superior preparation, whereas many of my worst failures can be traced to a lack of preparation. This is an area in which I've personally experienced just how fine the line between stupendous success and colossal failure can be.

Two of the most important reasons for being prepared are that (1) circumstances continually change and (2) the chances of a deal closing are inversely proportional to the amount of time that elapses between a verbal agreement and a closing. In other words, being prepared puts you in a position to get the deal closed as quickly as possible.

## A Rare Defeat for Legalman

One of the big payoffs I was alluding to came in the late 1960s when I spent many months negotiating the purchase of a company from an indecisive principal. Every time I thought the deal was set, Legalman came up with one reason or another why his client shouldn't, or couldn't, go through with the deal. Legalman, of course, was well aware that he would no longer be in a position to siphon off legal fees from the company's coffers once the deal closed, so, to his credit, it was obvious that he intended to fight the sale to the bitter end. Absolutely no scheme or ploy was beneath him; shame or embarrassment was not even an issue.

Unfortunately for Legalman, because of my impeccable preparation I was always one step ahead of him, so, notwithstanding his treachery, we kept inching closer and closer to a closing. Finally, all documentation was in order and the deal was set to close at—of all places—the Pierre Hotel in New York. Because I so respected Legalman's tenacity and resourcefulness for coming up with more and more absurd reasons why the sale couldn't be accomplished, I went overboard to prepare for this particular closing. I played through a hundred different scenarios and reasons that Legalman might be inclined to use in an attempt to block the closing, or at least have it postponed. I had documentation piled to the ceiling, paper clips poised, and staplers ready to be thrust into action on a moment's notice. What I'm trying to say is: I was *ready*.

The reviewing of documents and stalling went on all afternoon, until Legalman finally was able to get a stay of execution by insisting on dinner. However, I was successful in convincing everyone that we should have dinner in the suite and keep right on reviewing documents. As the hours rolled by, I sensed that Legalman was getting to his client in subtle ways, and, sure enough, around 12:30 A.M., just after Legalman whispered something in his client's ear, the client got up and nervously announced, "I'm sorry, but I just can't go through with this." Whereupon he and his two top aides departed with Legalman. "End of deal," I thought. "What a great story this would make for a book."

After a philosophical discourse with *my* Legalman, I was just about ready to call it a night and write it off as just one of those things when the doorbell rang. Startled, I looked at my watch and saw that it was 1:30 A.M. I opened the door, and there, to my surprise, stood the seller and his entourage, including a very miffed-looking Legalman. The seller said, "You know, we walked around the block a few times, and I thought to myself, 'What am I afraid of, anyway?' I decided to act on my gut instincts and go through with the deal. Let's get on with the signing of the papers."

It's big moments like this when being prepared really pays off. Had Legalman been given enough time, I think he might have managed to swing the pendulum of doubt back in the other direction once more, which probably would have been its last swing on this particular deal. But once I got the go-ahead, I was in a position to move swiftly. Every document was in perfect order; even the pages were turned back to the spot where signatures were needed. Within minutes, all documents were signed, sealed, and delivered, and, just like that, the deal that had been off an hour before was now closed.

While it's true that life can be unfair, and that you cannot prevent the inevitable, it's also true that when the breaks do come your way, as they did for me that memorable night at the Pierre Hotel, you have to be prepared to take advantage of them. Remember, breaks float in and out of people's lives every day without being exploited.

## Your Greatest Ally

When I talk about being prepared in order to take advantage of the breaks, it's back to relying on the law of averages. If you believe in the law of averages—and, hopefully, that isn't even an issue by now—you know that it's just a matter of time until you get your share of the breaks. Time goes hand in hand with being prepared, and time is where your self-discipline is really put to the test. Time will always come to your rescue, providing you have the self-discipline to stay prepared. Patience isn't a virtue when it comes to getting results; it's a necessity. Once again, it's hard to improve on the words of Baltasar Gracián, who declared so simply, yet so profoundly, "Time and I against any other two."

The late Chinn Ho, the fabulously wealthy Hawaiian who was frequently referred to as the Chinese Rockefeller, once said in an interview that one of the secrets of his great financial success was that he practiced the philosophy "Wait long, then move fast." In other words, he had the self-discipline to wait for the right opportunity, then, when it arrived, he moved swiftly to take advantage of it.

Perhaps the epitome of demonstrating the wait-long-then-move-fast philosophy was demonstrated by the legendary Boston Red Sox slugger, Ted Williams. In the view of many, Williams was the greatest hitter of all time. In an article about Williams some years ago, he was reported as saying that in the course of a game he expected to see only one perfect pitch. Considering that a batter usually receives anywhere from twenty to fifty pitches per game, I found Williams's statement to be fascinating. He said that because he had no idea when that one perfect pitch would appear, he knew it was crucial to have the self-discipline to be both prepared and patient.

As a business philosophy, Williams's strategy is unbeatable.

Experience has convinced me that it never fails to pay big dividends over the long term.

## Part-time Versus Full-time Self-Discipline

There's a big difference between being self-disciplined in a certain situation at a certain time and being a self-disciplined person. Being a self-disciplined person is what the Self-Discipline Habit is all about. Anyone can display self-discipline on occasion, but to get consistently positive results takes consistency. It's the day-in, day-out practice of self-discipline that determines where you'll be at the end of a week, a month, a year, or a lifetime. Remember, a lifetime is nothing more than an accumulation of years, months, weeks, and days, and what takes place in those smaller increments of time will determine whether or not your life, on the whole, is successful.

If you aspire to play in the big leagues, you must be prepared to play every point as though it were match point. In other words, you have to be consistently focused. Dabblers are rarely, if ever, successful. It's when you focus totally, intensely, and consistently on one project—a project that has the potential to yield a worthwhile payoff—that you have the greatest chance for success.

You must have the self-discipline not to allow others to pull you off course with side projects or unrelated ventures. You must have the self-discipline to keep your mind from wandering toward thoughts of what else you should be doing, who slighted you last week, how you're going to clear up some bothersome financial problem, and a thousand and one other concerns that perpetually and randomly bombard your mind. You must make it a habit to block out those things that do not contribute to the creative process.

Anyone who has ever written a book knows that it cannot be done any other way but through controlled attention. Dispersed attention produces either a lot of unfinished books or books that *read* as if the writer's attention was dispersed. The most difficult project in the world is to start from a blank piece of paper every day, then have the self-discipline to stay with it for hours at a time without interruption. This is true of any profession, not just writing. Your success at getting results is directly tied to the number of hours you consistently devote to intense, uninterrupted, creative thinking. If you discipline yourself to do this four to six hours a day, you'll be astonished by the results. To paraphrase the turn-of-the-century advertising legend Claude Hopkins, what appears to be genius is often nothing more than "the art of taking pains."

## The Exception

Talk about inhabiting a world of delusions, the word *exception* itself is delusive because, in the real world, exceptions are rarely the nonrecurring phenomena that people would like to believe they are. In fact, the Self-Discipline Habit and The Exception are at opposite ends of the success spectrum.

Because it so graphically illustrates my point about The Exception, I'd like to use another nonbusiness example from my personal experience, one that again is equally applicable to the business world. Years ago I found out the hard way about the delusive nature of The Exception when I began rationalizing about my eating habits. It seemed that every day I was saying to myself, "Well, I've already blown it today, so I may as well enjoy myself." My rationalizations in this area came to an end after an episode I nostalgically refer to as the Battle of Little Big Pie.

Many years earlier I had pared more than fifty pounds off my Orson Welles look-alike body. Since that time, I had taken great care to watch my caloric intake and adhere to a vigorous exercise program. Then one day I allowed myself to make an exception . . . which was followed by another exception . . . which was followed by another . . . and another . . . and another. Just about the time my weight was beginning to get out of hand, I happened to go to Palm Springs for a quiet weekend. By that time I had renewed my old habit of nibbling. I nibbled everything in sight—candy, potato chips, tree bark, index cards—anything that fell into my path.

As I waddled down the streets of Palm Springs looking like The Thing, people screamed as I approached. However, I hadn't even scratched the surface of my caloric potential. My true, championship form didn't show itself until Saturday evening when I was having dinner with an old friend from the East Coast. As I ate my meal, panting and perspiring, my friend tactfully mentioned that it looked as if I had "put on a little weight." I suspected his remark was prompted by the fact that I had eaten all the bread on the table and had started to butter my left forefinger. Finally, I came right out with it: "I don't know how this got started, but lately I've been eating like a wild boar. Now I've already gone so far over the line that nothing else I eat tonight could make much difference. It's already a lost weekend, so I may as well go all the way."

That was the go-ahead signal. I totally deserted my self-discipline. You could hear the "Rocky" theme music in the background as I mounted a ground offensive against the kitchen. My friend and his wife trembled in awe, expressing fear, then disbelief, when at last I ordered dessert. The piece of coconut cream pie the waiter brought me must have been the largest portion ever served to a mammal west of the Rockies. I got the distinct feeling the waiter was mocking me. I remember my friend asking me, incredulously, "Are you going to eat that *whole thing?*" I was already disgusted with myself, so why not go for it? What difference would another few thousand calories make? I must immodestly tell you that it was an incredible finish, right out of the movie *Fatso*. Everyone in the restaurant who had thrilled to Dom DeLuise and his pals chanting in unison, "Get the honey," couldn't help but feel a twinge of excitement as my head fell forward into my plate. I had done it. I had gone the distance with that gargantuan piece of pie.

I awoke the next morning with a pounding foodover, and realized that it was either a return to no exceptions or back to the way things had been years before when my life had been devoid of self-discipline. The decision wasn't hard to make. One glance at an old picture of myself was all it took. In that worn-out, crumpled photo, I looked like an experiment gone wrong—a corpulent cross between Wimpy and Sidney Greenstreet. I mean to tell you, I was big. They say no man is an island, but I came close. And why not? In the old days, I had set world records in the freestyle banana-split competition and the wind-aided buttered-popcorn dash. The way I ate, I was lucky the universe was expanding.

After the Palm Springs eatfest, I caught hold of myself and admitted that my exceptions had again become the rule. Eating out of disgust was once more becoming a way of life. I got just close enough to my old self to get a glimpse of what the long-term consequences would be if I kept it up. Beginning the next day it was back to a delightful life of consistency, no exceptions, and liking myself again. Best of all, I escaped my old niche of being a perennial contender for the Fatty Arbuckle Award and began having delusions of grandeur when I looked in the mirror. "Eat your heart out, Arnold," I thought to myself as I flexed my awesome three-inch biceps.

### PUTTING THE FUN BACK IN LIFE

Through the process of association, the experience I just related to you has paid big dividends in helping me to avoid exceptions in my business life, particularly when it comes to creative projects. I now find little difficulty concentrating for hours at a time without a break.

The problem with The Exception can be summed up best by **Real-World Rule No. 28: Every exception a person makes brings him closer to a life where the exception becomes the rule, until life itself becomes one big exception.** About all you can say about such an individual is that he leads a very exceptional life.

Isn't it true that there's always a special game, a special event, or a special circumstance to tempt you? And isn't there always someone around to chide you, "Aw, c'mon, just this one time.

What's the big deal? It's not going to kill you." Maybe it won't kill you, but, little by little, exceptions will destroy your life. So it's at those moments when you're being most pressured to make exceptions that you find out just how strong your self-discipline really is. The question is, is it strong enough for you to look the other person in the eye unflinchingly and say "No!" without hesitation?

I realize that some people might argue that being self-disciplined to the point of trying to eliminate all exceptions leads to a grim existence. However, I've found just the opposite to be true. I feel the more you like to play, the *more* self-disciplined you should be. Why? Because if you understand that there's no such thing as something for nothing, you'll be anxious to pay now so you can play later—without the Guilt Fairy looking over your shoulder and watching your every move.

It's not a matter of being perfect; rather, it's a matter of *striving* for perfection. Just because you never can be perfect doesn't mean you shouldn't *try* to do your best. That means that when you do weaken—when you do make an exception—you should try not to delude yourself about it. Instead, acknowledge that it happened and cut your losses before they get out of hand. Catch yourself before you go from bad to worse; one more exception *will* hurt. Just because you had a bad morning at the office doesn't mean you should squander the rest of the day. Anyone can do well on good days, but only truly successful people—people who adhere to the Self-Discipline Habit—consistently make headway on bad days. No matter how many exceptions you've already made on a bad day, making one more isn't going to make matters better. It will, however, make them *worse*. Develop the habit of turning bad days, bad weeks, and bad months around by having the self-discipline to stop yourself *before* things get out of hand.

Positive results make life more enjoyable, and the Self-Discipline Habit leads to positive results. The bottom line, then, is that the Self-Discipline Habit leads to a more enjoyable life. And to be a self-disciplined person, as opposed to being occasionally self-disciplined, you can't coast. You've got to do it *every day*.

# Chapter 10

# The Action Habit

Theodore Roosevelt once confessed, "There is nothing brilliant nor outstanding in my record, except perhaps this one thing: I do the things that I believe ought to be done. . . . And when I make up my mind to do a thing, I act."

Without the Action Habit, the other nine major success habits I've covered in this book aren't of much use. Until action is taken, they are little more than theory, because results are not possible without action. Theories are nice, but ultimately they have to be implemented. The very state of being alive implies action.

In the first chapter I pointed out that one of the basic realities of life is that knowledge without wisdom is useless. A still more frustrating reality of life is that even if you possess knowledge *and* wisdom, the two of them together are useless without action. This is the other side of the preparedness coin. Everything in life works better in moderation, and too much preparation can become an excuse for indefinitely postponing action. In other words, you have to avoid falling in love with planning and strategizing to the extreme that it becomes an end in itself. No matter how much planning you do, it's impossible to project solutions to most day-to-day problems.

I had a friend who was absolutely enamored with working on

projections for a great idea he had for a service business. He worked away on his computer for two years, and while circumstances continued to change regarding the industry he was planning to enter, he kept right on revising his projections. One day I visited him and was puzzled by the excitement he displayed. He had just revised his figures again, and said, "Can you believe what these computer programs can do? Watch this: If I change just one figure in my projected cash-flow chart, all the other figures change instantaneously. Isn't that unbelievable?"

To which I responded, "Yes, it's great—but you're going broke."

My friend had allowed himself to get sidetracked by something I discussed earlier: confusing the means with the end. He had become so carried away with his computer's capacity, not to mention his own computer skills, that he had forgotten his original objective. It was not to become an expert at doing cash-flow projections; it was to find a way to convert his idea into a profitable enterprise. Planning is a vital, first step to getting results, but it can never be a substitute for action. You can't reach second base if you never take your foot off first base.

You've often heard the expression "Ideas are a dime a dozen." Yet an idea can change the world—and many have. All that is meant by the dime-a-dozen cliché is that an idea, by itself, has no intrinsic value. It must be accompanied by action. In this respect, an idea really is the first step in the success chain, with preparation and planning comprising the second, and action the third.

I like to half-jokingly tell audiences that I "invented" Federal Express. And it's true. However, I'm sure that thousands of other entrepreneurs and would-be entrepreneurs did, too. When I was attempting to put deals together all over the country during the late 1960s, continually fighting deadlines and trying to get documents to distant cities as quickly as possible, it occurred to me that it would be a great service business to offer overnight delivery of important papers to people like myself. In fact, I thought about it off and on for years . . . while someone named Fred Smith came along and actually did it.

The moral is to be found in an old adage that says: The successful implementation of one good idea is worth more than a thousand good ideas not acted upon.

Who wants to *invent* Federal Express? I'd much rather own it.

## Roadblocks to Making Things Happen

To develop the Action Habit you have to overcome the mental obstacles that *prevent* people from taking action. I've already discussed the most fundamental reason of all for failing to take action: lack of a meaning to life. Whenever you feel inertia (the disinclination to act) overtaking you, you should go back to the five Present Living Questions discussed in Chapter 4.

The last suggestion I made in that chapter was to step back and review your progress periodically, and if you don't seem to be getting where you want to be in life, reevaluate your answers. If you haven't answered the Present Living Questions honestly, or if circumstances have changed in such a way as to make your original answers invalid, it's easy to slip into a state of inertia and feel as if there's no reason to get up in the morning. If you do feel confident that your answers remain valid—which should manifest itself as a strong inner desire to achieve one or more objectives—yet something seems to be preventing you from taking action, the answer probably lies in searching for other obstacles that may be stifling you, then finding ways to deal with those obstacles.

In analyzing my own periods of inaction over the years, I've come up with six major roadblocks to making things happen, all of which are primarily mental in nature. That's an exciting realization, because it means that freeing yourself from an action-jam is primarily a mind problem, and mind problems can always be resolved.

In other words, once the mental obstacle is removed, action follows almost automatically. Even more exciting is the fact that, as with the other major success habits discussed in this book, the Action Habit doesn't require superior intelligence or specialized skills. It requires only the will to cultivate the habit of making things happen.

## Obstacle No. 1: Resistance to Change

Homeostasis, the tendency to cling to the status quo, or to existing conditions, and avoid change is a common human trait. Unfortunately, it is also a self-defeating and self-destructive habit. Of all the negative things that can be said about the phenomenon of homeostasis, the worst is that it defies the laws of Nature. The reality is that life *is* change, from the generation and dying of cells in your body to the construction and demolition of buildings in a city. Weather changes; laws change; the economy changes; the reigns of power change; technology changes; and, perhaps most significantly of all, your age changes every second of your life.

I thought a lot about this problem at a young age, because I was acutely aware of my own resistance to change. I concluded that at the heart of the problem was fear—fear of the unknown. We all grow comfortable with existing conditions, even those we dislike. For sheer physical discomfort, the worst experience of my life was serving in the Army. I never had been away from home for any significant length of time prior to my unpleasant Army experience, yet the phenomenon of homeostasis took hold of me during my tour of duty. I was in the artillery, the one branch of the military in which continual uprooting, moving, and digging in at new locations is a given. Constant state of change is a way of life in the artillery.

Artillery personnel are trained to treat each new position as a permanent home because their length of stay in any given location is always unknown. It could be as little as ten minutes or as long as ten weeks. What surprised me was that each time we pitched our tents and got settled, I mentally resisted uprooting again. I remember one stretch in particular when we stayed in the same area of snow-covered mountains for over a week in zero-degree weather. My tent became home to me, and I "set up house" as comfortably as possible. I'll never forget the mental twinge I felt when we were ordered to break down our tents, gather our gear, and move out. As miserable and cold as it was in the mountains, I actually had become accustomed to my little routine.

If something as inherently unpleasant as sleeping in a tent—in the mountains, in snow and cold, in the Army—can become comfortable to someone, it's easy to see why we become accustomed to situations in everyday life that are nowhere near as bleak. As a result, people get stuck in dead-end jobs, professions they dislike, and other conditions that make their lives miserable. What usually keeps them from taking life-changing action is fear of the unknown. To overcome such fear, the first thing you must do is accept the reality that circumstances surrounding your life will change *regardless* of whether or not you want them to. The only unknowns are how and when. It's up to you to decide whether you want to direct the changes, or whether you're content to react to them. The problem with the latter approach is that it leads to a lack of control, which *never* leads to positive results. Always remember: That which you can confront you can control; that which you cannot confront will control you.

Finally, it's a matter of how you frame the phenomenon of change in your mind. If you think of change as the essence of life, as an exciting, integral part of the living experience, you can wipe fear from your consciousness. Best of all, I've found this to be a relatively easy thing to accomplish, because experience has taught me that change *is* exciting. I never cease to be amazed when I look back on my life and see how many major changes have taken place in a relatively short period of time, and how most of them have been for the better.

Put another way, if change is inevitable—and it is—why not assign it a positive rather than a negative value? By so doing, you'll find that it will be much easier for you to develop the

Action Habit and to be able to control much of the change that takes place in your life.

## Obstacle No. 2: Waiting for Something to Happen

As mentioned earlier, many people naïvely assume that everyone else is vitally interested in their affairs. Unfortunately, it simply isn't so. In business, in particular, it's important to come to grips with the reality that no one cares about your deal as much as you do.

Perhaps you've noticed that if you have something the other party wants, your phone will ring off the hook. But if you need cooperation from the other party to get a deal closed that's more important to you than to him, you're lucky if he'll return your calls. Talk about facing reality, like it or not, that's the way the real world works. It's also the reason that when you're on pins and needles and ready to close a deal, your investor mysteriously goes on vacation for two weeks without giving you advance notice, your accountant leaves for the day to play golf, and Legalman frantically searches his little black book to find someone to treat him to lunch (and, at the same time, allow himself to be billed for the honor).

The point is that the more you have on the line, the more it's up to you to take action—to make things happen—because no one else cares. It's always safest to assume that your deal is important only to you. When you fall into the lethargic habit of waiting for others to take action on your behalf, you're doomed to disappointment. **Real-World Rule No. 64: If you want something to happen, *make it happen*.**

In discussing the concept of value for value, I suggested that if you want more, you should make yourself worth more. However, I certainly didn't mean to imply that everyone with whom you deal will insist that you get your maximum reward. If you get results for people, that puts you in a *position* to ask for more. In most cases, however, you still have to take the initiative and *tell* people what you think you're worth.

In other words, you shouldn't naïvely assume that others will see to it that you receive maximum remuneration. Even if the other party is value-for-value oriented, that doesn't mean he has omniscient powers to recognize your true value. While you have to be careful not to overvalue what you bring to the table, it's also up to you to make it a regular habit to ask for what you're worth. **Real-World Rule No. 134: All other things being equal, the mere act of asking can be the main difference between one person's success and another person's mediocre station in life.**

I first thought about this principle when a friend of mine (some of whose trials and tribulations I discussed in Chapter 2), who was an attorney specializing in securing cable television franchises, told me about the evolution of his career. For years he was just a normal deal-killing attorney—drafting unintelligible legal documents and having three-martini lunches at the expense of his clients—until one day he decided to ask for what he thought he was worth. Until then he had charged his clients an hourly rate, but he made up his mind that he was going to up his fee by asking for a percentage of each deal in addition.

Sure enough, he convinced the next client who walked through the door that it was in the client's best interest to give Legalman a piece of his deal. It not only gave Legalman an incentive to get the results the client wanted, but to get them quickly. It's enough to take one's breath away to contemplate Legalman not having to spend the majority of his time trying to figure out how to kill his client's deal. Attorney haters will hate this, but, within a few years, Legalman ended up owning varying percentages of numerous cable television stations and became very wealthy—all because he had the courage to ask for what he thought he was worth.

**Real-World Rule No. 65: When you depend on no one but yourself, not only can you can never be disappointed, you also increase the chances of controlling your destiny.** It's foolhardy to sit back and wait for things to happen. The wise person cultivates the habit of *making things happen*.

## Obstacle No. 3: Feeling Overwhelmed

One of life's great frustrations is that the number of projects we would like to undertake is infinite, yet time is a limiting factor. The result is that we often feel overwhelmed and end up doing nothing. Strange, isn't it? We think that so much action is required that it results in our taking *no* action.

Like most people, throughout life I've wrestled hard with feeling overwhelmed by endless projects that continually demand my attention. Sometimes I feel like I'm in a nightmare, standing in the middle of a room with no doors or windows and a hundred projects piled on tables around the perimeter, all simultaneously screaming at me, "Do me first! Do me first!" If I so much as nod in the direction of any one project, all the other projects in the room become violent and start picketing with signs that read: RINGER UNFAIR TO URGENT PROJECTS.

Although it's impossible to totally eliminate the problem, even the most compulsive among us can take steps to ease it. In this regard, there are two basic realities that I think are essential to absorb.

First, given that time is a limited commodity, it really *isn't* possible to get everything done. Rest assured, however, that you are not alone. Everyone has time problems; no one gets everything done. How, then, does a successful person differ from an unsuccessful person in disposing of projects? A successful person consistently does the things *that need to be done* to achieve positive results, results that give the highest possible quality to his life. Remember the sign on my wall: Does it matter? If so, how *much* does it matter? Action is not an end-all, be-all. It takes *intelligent* action to achieve meaningful results. Don't fall into the trap of trying to substitute energy for reason.

The second important reality is that the compulsion to get everything done has no logical basis. *Why* do you need to get everything done? Is it possible that our obsession with wanting to get our lives neatly filed away is nothing more than an unconscious preparation for dying? If so, forget it. You can spend a lifetime chasing the elusive dream of having every aspect of your life in order, but to no avail. This, too, is a tough one for compulsives like me to swallow, but the reality is that the day you die you'll probably still have about the same number of projects left undone as you did the day you suffered your first attack of overwhelm.

Using these two realities as a foundation, I've successfully developed some simple action steps that enable me to handle the sense of feeling overwhelmed almost as well as a normal person. (Well, at least as well as a seminormal person.) I've made it a habit to implement these steps at the first sign of feeling overwhelmed. They never fail to alleviate any temporary state of paralysis I may be experiencing, and they always succeed in quickly getting me into an action mode. This is your lucky day, because you get the formula at no extra charge. All I ask is that you send me 10 percent of the increased peace of mind you experience during the first year of its use (providing, of course, that this doesn't constitute the sale of unregistered securities in your state).

**Step Number One.** At the first sign of feeling overwhelmed, call time-out and mentally and physically come to a complete stop.

**Step Number Two.** Stand back and get a big-picture perspective of the battlefield. This makes it much easier to objectively analyze the real—not imagined—downside consequences if you should fail to complete any given project on time, or fail to complete it at all. Always ask yourself, "So what?" And be honest about your answer in terms of a potential worst-case scenario. If the downside doesn't involve death or terminal illness, I lean hard on myself to keep it in proper perspective.

**Step Number Three.** Eliminate everything that isn't crucial to achieving your most important objectives. To accomplish this you have to resign yourself to some people being upset with you, but you can't allow yourself to be intimidated by others. It's important to mentally prepare yourself to make hard decisions, decisions that won't necessarily be popular with everyone. Remember, however, that unless such people are willing to do your work for you, it's they who are out of line with their display of displeasure.

**Step Number Four.** Don't try to do everything; just do *something*. If you don't learn to take life one wave at a time, it will overwhelm you. The aphorism "the only way to eat an elephant is one bite at a time" is all too appropriate. Remember, you'll never get everything done, so discipline yourself to prioritize. And since circumstances constantly change, always consider present conditions when setting priorities, then let those priorities determine your actions.

**Step Number Five.** Begin. So simple, yet this is what the problem of feeling overwhelmed—of failing to take action—is all about. At some point you actually have to do it, and the first step is almost always the hardest. In this respect, another maxim that is helpful is: A journey of a thousand miles begins with the first step.

**Step Number Six.** Concentrate exclusively on the project at hand. This is where you need to call on your self-discipline. If you've already decided that something is the most important thing for you to work on right now, respect your own decision by ignoring the 7,328 other projects that you'd also like to get done. No matter how pressing the second-most important project may be, it's not quite as important as the one you're presently working on. The only way you'll ever be able to give project number two your complete attention is to first concentrate fully on project number one.

**Step Number Seven.** Sustain your movement at a comfortable pace. I've referred to this in past writings as the "slow, fast way." The frantic approach doesn't work. Again, self-discipline is required. I'm often amazed at how much I manage to accomplish in an hour's time when I just calm down and work at a modest pace. The results of this philosophy show up most glaringly in a lack of mistakes, because nothing is more time consuming than having to go back and redo something.

**Step Number Eight.** Don't stop until you're done. Remember some of the rules we've already discussed: Look the pass into your hands; you're not through till you've crossed all the t's and dotted all the i's and the check has cleared the bank; it ain't over till it's over; etc., etc., etc. In our world of delusions, I've long been fascinated by how so many people have a habit of announcing that they're done with something, yet, on closer inspection, it often turns out that they aren't even close to being done. Apparently it makes them feel better if they can just *say* they're done. Don't delude yourself in this area. Learn to go the last five yards—and kick the extra point—before telling anyone, especially yourself, that you're done.

**Step Number Nine.** Then, and only then, move on to the next project. This is really an exclamation point on Step Number Eight. Unless you're *completely* done, don't start working on project number two, or, worse, on an even less important project. If you start dabbling in the next project before you're finished with the current one, you'll succeed only in stepping right back into the Overwhelm Trap.

## Obstacle No. 4: The Time Is Never Right

Talk about a procrastinator's dream, this is it—probably the most insidious of all obstacles to taking action. If you're waiting for everything to be just right before taking action, you are in possession of a foolproof excuse for failure. **Real-World Rule No. 111: Conditions are never right at the right time; the timing is *always* wrong.**

When people cling to the excuse that the time isn't right to do something, it's often because, as mentioned earlier, they are emotionalizing the word *hard* and confusing it with the word *impossible*. It's not impossible to change occupations right now; just hard. It's not impossible to move to another city right now; just hard. It's not impossible to terminate a bad partnership right now; just hard. The tendency to see *hard* as *impossible* is closely tied to the tendency to resist change. Don't delude yourself into believing that just because something is hard, it's impossible.

In addition to its close connection to the problem of resistance to change, confusing hard with impossible is often tied to a trait I discussed in association with good human relations: flexibility. It's important to understand that the opportunity available to you at any given time will never be the perfect opportunity. Again, life doesn't work that way. The inability to cope with the imperfections of life leads only to frustration and inaction.

While it's a healthy perspective to believe that the best deal in the world comes along every day, it's equally healthy to acknowledge that there's no such thing as a perfect deal. There are times when the deal that's available to you may just be the deal you need at that moment. An acquaintance of mine once told me that a year prior to his being named president of CBS Radio, he accepted a job as general manager of a CBS Radio affiliate station in Sacramento, California. When I asked him how in the world he had found himself in such an unglamorous position just twelve months before achieving the top spot at CBS Radio, he replied, "Let me just say that the job I took in Sacramento wasn't the deal I wanted, but, due to a variety of personal circumstances, it was the deal I *needed* at that particular time."

Above all, don't allow yourself to be lulled into the New Year's Resolution Syndrome, rationalizing away each wasted day by thinking, "I'm going to work on improving my efficiency starting the first of the year," or, "I'm going to start making ten sales calls a day beginning next month," or, "I'm going to start working on that project as soon as I get everything else under control." The New Year's Resolution Syndrome is a first cousin to The Exception. It's the antithesis of living in the present, and leads only to a life of endless procrastination.

The time to start becoming efficient is *today*. The time to make a sales call is *today*. The time to start working on a project is *today*. And the time to start picking up the pieces and begin over again is *today*. Develop the habit of living in the present. The best day really is today, so get started now, no matter what your problems are and no matter how long you've already procrastinated.

## Obstacle No. 5: Self-Doubt

Self-doubt is a much more common problem than many people would like to believe. I am convinced that, to one extent or another, everyone—and I do mean everyone—harbors self-doubt. It's a trait we're handed with our birth certificate.

The average person has a bigger-than-life view of great athletes, show-business celebrities, and other public figures, and, as a result, has a difficult time picturing them as mere mortals. Nonetheless, having known many public figures through the years, I can testify that their generally inflated images are grossly inaccurate. Some of the most insecure people I've known are outrageously wealthy, extremely famous, or both.

Bob Cousy, the legendary ex-Boston Celtic guard, once said in an interview, ". . . even the great [athletes] choke at one point or another. The ones that deny it are liars. They're lying to themselves and they're lying to the public." These are surprising words, coming from a former superstar athlete noted for his clutch performances. Arguably, the reason a great athlete chokes is that he, at least subconsciously, loses confidence; or, to put it in corollary terms, he gets a rush of self-doubt at the moment of truth. Realizing that people we look up to also harbor self-doubt helps to put the matter in proper perspective.

Just knowing that you're not alone, that you're not some kind of freak because you sometimes experience a twinge of self-doubt, can serve as a good first step toward overcoming the problem.

A second aid in overcoming self-doubt is to ask yourself, "What are the downside consequences if I should fail to accomplish my objective?" It's important to remember that events rarely turn out to be anywhere near as bad as we picture them. Continually reminding yourself to analyze honestly and objectively what might be the worst-case consequences of a failure goes a long way toward reducing self-doubt. Objective analysis usually reveals that self-doubt is based more on emotion than reality.

Third, we live in a very negative world, a world in which we continually meet people who try to convince us that what we want to do can't be done. In truth, every successful person in history has been told—many times—that what he wanted to accomplish couldn't be done. In an article about Fred Astaire the day after he died, I was amused by a quote from a critic's review early in Astaire's career: "Can't act. Can't sing. Balding. Can dance a little." Such is the story of life. The important question is whether or not a person will allow such negative input to prevent him from taking action.

Unfortunately, most people do allow the continual barrage of negative input from others to render them immobile. When people repeatedly bombard our heads with negative mental darts, it's very difficult to keep from thinking, "Maybe they're right. Maybe I can't do it." It's another one of those vicious cycles: The more you hear that you can't accomplish something, the more self-doubt you have; and the more self-doubt you have, the easier target you are for those who thrive on negatives. And this kind of cycle *can* lead to failure if you don't make it a habit to short-circuit it as quickly as possible.

Finally, to overcome self-doubt you must face the reality that you *will* fail—often and in a big way. This is where the Natural Law of Balance and the law of averages again come into play.

No matter how long you wait, no matter how much you try to prepare yourself, you're still going to make mistakes. It's one of those inevitabilities of life, a reality of being human.

Knowing this, I've developed a trick that I play on my mind, one that conditions it to look at action as an opportunity to *practice* making mistakes. If you've read the biographies of many famous people, you know that the path to greatness is always strewn with mistakes and failures. I'm convinced that one way in which superachievers become great is by learning through their mistakes. In the words of Richard Bach, "That's what learning is, after all: not whether we lose the game, but how we lose and how we've changed because of it, and what we take away from it that we never had before, to apply to other games. Losing, in a curious way, is winning."

I thought about the wisdom of Bach's words when a friend of mine, Marsh Fisher, told me the remarkable story of how he and his partner built Century 21 Real Estate into an international success. Through most of his life, Marsh was like millions of other would-be entrepreneurs, trying his hand at a number of occupations, but never quite finding his niche. He kicked around from one venture to another until, at age forty-four, he became involved in a franchise venture in the San Fernando Valley area of Los Angeles. However, after about two years of tough going, the company failed.

Marsh then came up with a new franchising idea, one that he believed would lead to a megasuccess. He spent about two years trying to find someone to back his idea, until finally, at age forty-seven, he got someone to put up $6,000 to help get it off the ground. Within six months, Marsh Fisher's new company was able to sell about sixty franchises in Southern California, even though it had virtually no working capital, no experience, no existing franchises to display as models, and no fancy brochures or literature.

Within a few short years, Marsh Fisher's company, Century 21 Real Estate, became a household name, and his brainchild was purchased by Trans World Airlines for $89 million. A few years after that, TWA sold the company to Prudential Life Insurance for $250 million.

The first lesson here is that an idea, when coupled with action, can indeed be a very powerful force. But what I found most significant about Marsh Fisher's story is when he told me, "If I hadn't first tried and failed in the franchising venture in the San Fernando Valley, there's absolutely no way I and my partner could have made a success of Century 21. The things I learned the first time around were the key to Century 21's success."

The mistakes Marsh Fisher made in his first franchising venture were unpleasant, to be sure, but they were necessary to learn what he needed to know to win over the long term. This, I am convinced, is an important key to overcoming self-doubt. You must develop the habit of thinking of mistakes as opportunities to learn and grow. With that kind of perspective, it then becomes much easier to take action.

## Obstacle No. 6: Adversity

In discussing self-doubt as an obstacle to action, I was referring primarily to the individual who is afraid to take the first step, who can never quite bring himself to leave the starting gate. Adversity, however, is a different kind of obstacle. When I speak of adversity as an obstacle to action, I'm referring to the individual who has taken action—perhaps many times—but, because of obstacles, rejection, bad luck, and/or disappointment over lack of results, has become too discouraged to continue. Though I used Marsh Fisher's story to illustrate how viewing mistakes as learning opportunities can help a person to overcome self-doubt, his story also is a classic example of overcoming adversity.

It's essential to be able to overcome adversity as an obstacle to taking action, because, without exception, there's no such thing as success without adversity. As I pointed out earlier, no matter how well things may be going for you at any given time, fortune tires of carrying anyone on its shoulders too long. Problems are inevitable. Life often seems to be a perpetual attempt to fit square pegs into round holes.

The essential trait needed to overcome adversity is perseverance, most of the ingredients for which are to be found in the first nine chapters of this book. Perseverance requires knowledge and wisdom. In particular, it requires a clear understanding of the reality that problems are an integral, ongoing part of life; of the Natural Law of Balance; of the law of averages; and of the power of the mind to determine, to a great extent, one's destiny. To the degree a person possesses an understanding of these realities, he demonstrates belief, which in turn leads to an expansive mental paradigm (which, for all practical purposes, is synonymous with having a positive mental attitude). Also, it's important to remember that an expansive mental paradigm represents a resourceful, or alternative-thinking, mind, a mind that continually searches for new solutions no matter what kind of roadblocks confront it.

To be motivated to carry on in the face of adversity, an individual needs desire, which comes about as a result of correctly answering the Present Living Questions discussed in Chapter 4. The answers to these questions give meaning to a person's life, which in turn gives him the desire to keep going in spite of obstacles, opposition, discouragement, and bad luck. Adversity, then, tests your commitment to your goals. Plain and simple, the probability of success in any venture is increased in direct proportion to your willingness to keep going in spite of obstacles. If you want something badly enough, you won't give up; if not, you will. It might be appropriate to say that an expansive mental paradigm and desire are the father and mother of perseverance.

Finally, two other ingredients that we've already discussed—time and focus—determine the *degree* of an individual's perseverance. To persevere over the long term, you have to have the self-discipline to keep focused on your main objective and to be patient until things finally come together for you.

Given what's involved; it's easy to understand why most people do not display a great deal of perseverance. That's unfortunate, considering that perseverance probably is the most powerful success tool known to man. Perseverance is the ultimate manifestation of the Action Habit, because it is *continual* action. Perseverance means being able to handle massive rejection, massive disappointment, and massive frustration. It's what makes you persist long after the other guy has given up. In fact, if you stop to think about it, no one can defeat you. Defeat can occur only when *you* decide to quit. And the nice thing about it is that there's no limit to the number of times you can try.

Perseverance is a trait so powerful that it can overcome almost any deficiency. It will always put you at an advantage over the individual with more brains or talent, because neither intelligence nor skill is involved. Personally, I've never tried to kid myself about my IQ or skills. There have been very few days in my life when I haven't met someone who is far smarter and/or far more talented than I am. Whatever success I've managed to achieve, I attribute to being perhaps the most relentless, resilient, perseverant individual I know. I practice simple success habits on a regular basis—success habits that are accessible to everyone—and so long as I maintain the self-discipline to keep focused, these habits never fail me. Admittedly, it's not as attention-getting as being a person gifted with special talents, but the idea is to play the hand you're dealt as best you can. Remember, it's what you *do* with what you *have*.

As with the obstacle of feeling overwhelmed, over the years I've developed a systematic approach to handling adversity, steps that you, too, can easily implement whenever you feel as though obstacles are jamming your action gears.

**Step Number One.** Never take the attitude "Well, at least things can't get any worse." Trust me, they can! While it's nice to be unperturbable, it's also unwise to be too cavalier when adversity strikes. It's important to move swiftly into action, particularly if the adversity has disaster implications.

**Step Number Two.** As with the problem of feeling over-whelmed, call time out and mentally and physically come to a complete stop. Panic is an irrational, quick-spreading fear. If you're irrational, your perception of reality is warped. As a re-sult, panic tends to promote short-term relief at the expense of long-term success.

**Step Number Three.** Stop the hemorrhaging. This means min-imizing the damage, which you do by stabilizing the situation as quickly as possible. In financial terms, it means avoiding throw-ing good money after bad.

**Step Number Four.** Again, as with feeling overwhelmed, stand back and get a big-picture perspective of the battlefield. Is this really a life-and-death matter? Are you, or is anyone in your family, terminally ill? And even if it is a genuine disaster, is it possible to pick up the pieces and start over again?

**Step Number Five.** In a rigidly self-disciplined manner, focus exclusively on the crux of the problem. To do this, you have to eliminate all excess baggage. Simply refuse to make exceptions for anyone or anything. Firmly stick to your guns and have the courage to say *no* to everyone. If someone tries to get you to take your eye off the ball—like trying to coax you into watching Monday Night Football—just look him in the eye and calmly say, "Sorry, I'd love to, but I'm being executed in the morning."

**Step Number Six.** Carefully and honestly analyze the problem in terms of what *you* did wrong. It's essential that you not focus on what others did. In other words, avoid the delusion of trans-ference. To the extent you blame others, you succeed only in evading the real issue and thereby make it virtually impossible to figure out what *you* have to do—not only to solve the problem at hand, but to see that it never happens again. Also, to a responsible person there's no such thing as mitigating circum-stances. A so-called mitigating circumstance is really just a *rea-*

*son* why something happened to you, but it doesn't excuse you from the fact that *you* allowed it to happen. Develop the habit of figuring out what *you* did wrong so you can get on with doing something about it.

**Step Number Seven.** Start moving in the right direction as quickly as possible. Concentrate on maximizing the positives of the situation and implementing long-term, permanent solutions in order to avoid setting up still more balloon notes for yourself down the road. Forget about the adversity you've just experienced—let go of it—and get on with your life. This may involve making major changes, because extreme problems often call for extreme solutions.

As you can see, applying the Action Habit to the problem of adversity is a mental task that requires hard work. It's clear that there's only one way to handle a crisis effectively, and that's to meet it head-on. You learn to solve problems by dealing with them, not by running away.

Finally, it's helpful to view adversity in proper perspective. As unpleasant as adversities are, they're really just opportunities to grow, and personal growth leads to long-term success. Thus, failure acts as a process-of-elimination device in that each failure brings us one step closer to success. You can't afford to let up, because you never know when you might be just one step away from victory. As you've seen throughout this book, the practice of alternative thinking and the Natural Law of Balance make adversity little more than future success masquerading as failure. In addition, the Natural Law of Balance assures us that the longer we work to achieve something, the more meaningful it becomes.

## The Greatest of All Dangers

The most important lesson to be learned from this chapter is that taking no action is the greatest danger of all. Remember, even inaction is a form of action—passive action—and therefore has consequences. The problem, however, is that you don't control those consequences; they are consequences by default. In other words, if you don't take the initiative, events will control *you*. That in turn means that you will be *reacting* instead of *acting*.

Another old maxim says that you have to take a chance to get a chance. No matter how successful you may be in cultivating the nine other major success habits discussed in previous chapters, it's all for naught if you don't take action. The Action Habit literally is a life-and-death matter: Life is action; death is inaction. You'll have plenty of time for the latter at some (hopefully) far-off future time.

## The Choice Is Yours

I emphasize again that there is no big secret to success, that achieving positive results has little to do with superior intelligence or special skills of any kind, and that formal education, hard work, and luck are incidental to an individual's place on the success ladder. The chances are that you're already a lot closer to getting where you want to be in life than you realize. Remember, the difference between stupendous success and colossal failure is remarkably small.

The choice is yours: You can spend your time hoping to find the mysterious secret to success that eludes the average person throughout life, or you can put your efforts into cultivating the same simple habits that all successful people routinely practice. I personally can guarantee you that the latter is the most certain way to win big over the long term. One last time: *Success is not a grand-slam home run.*

As I stated in the Introduction, two realities make the philosophy of Million Dollar Habits a very exciting proposition: First, it works; second, these habits can be learned by anyone who is willing to put forth the necessary effort. The operative word here is *effort*. While these habits are simple enough to learn, to practice them requires a serious, constant output of energy.

Is there another alternative? Yes. If practicing Million Dollar Habits sounds like too much work, you always have the option of choosing to live a completely tranquil life. After all, tranquility is just a lobotomy away.

. . . to be continued.

# Index

Inquiries regarding Robert Ringer's availability to speak to your group, meeting, conference, or convention should be addressed to:

## SEMINAR CENTER, LTD.
## P. O. BOX 09724
## COLUMBUS, OHIO 43209

## (614) 236-1703